"One of the questions I have foun~~d~~ reclaim the ancient idea of the c~~o~~ how can we respond in a way that ~~promotes and~~ preserves our best values? Using the backdrop of disaster preparedness, this book tells how individuals, congregations, and communities have worked together to respond in times of tragedy and crisis. It is a great resource for people of faith to know how best to love and serve their neighbors."
— Jim Wallis, Sojourners

"I am delighted to hear about the release of *Help and Hope: Disaster Preparedness and Response Tools for Congregations.* When I read through the list of contributing writers, I knew the text would be rich with 'best known solutions.' The diverse experience of the writers have experienced firsthand the importance of preparing congregations, and I strongly recommend all faith leaders invest in the time to read the wisdom imparted within the text."
— Jono Anzalone, The American Red Cross

"As people of faith, we are compelled to heal a hurting world. However, it is more apparent than ever that we need strong relationships and the proper tools to accomplish this. Church World Service is a leader in this effort, training faith based partners in disaster preparedness, response, and recovery. *Help and Hope* is yet another example of this worthwhile and timely effort, providing direction and advice to those congregations who wish to prepare for ministry to those affected by disaster."
— Keith Adams, Episcopal Dioceses of New Jersey and Newark

"*Help and Hope* is a much-needed resource that has been long-awaited. Penned by skilled ministers and practitioners, this practical guide is for both ordained and lay ministers alike. Here you glimpse the gritty work of post-trauma ministry through real-life illustrations, useful questions that lead to actionable next steps, and roadmaps for planning meaningful worship, practicing care, and envisioning mission after trauma. If you and your congregation are discerning your roles in the aftermath of disaster, this will be a helpful companion. More books like this one are needed in the coming years as congregations continue to embrace their capacities to be catalysts for healing after trauma."
— Kate Wiebe, Institute for Congregational Trauma and Growth (ICTG) and Presbyterian Disaster Assistance (PDA)

Help AND HOPE

DISASTER PREPAREDNESS AND RESPONSE TOOLS FOR CONGREGATIONS

AMY GOPP
BRANDON GILVIN
EDS.

CHALICE
PRESS
ST. LOUIS, MISSOURI

Cover art: iStock photo.
Cover design: Scribe, Inc.

www.chalicepress.com

Print: 9780827214989   EPUB: 9780827214996   EPDF: 9780827215009

Library of Congress Cataloging in Publication data available upon request

Printed in the United States of America

Contents

Providing the Eye in the Storm: Perspectives on Psychosocial Care and Disaster Response

The Congregational Toolkit: Community Resources

Worship Materials

Foreword

Help and Hope: Disaster Preparedness and Response Tools for Congregations is an indispensable tool for faith communities to prepare for the critical role they can play when disasters impact their hometowns. This resource provides what the disaster relief and emergency response field has been missing and what North American communities of faith have needed— guidance on how to be an asset rather than an obstacle when assisting those who have been affected by disaster.

Twice when I was a teenager, my family's home and business suffered major damage from flooding and high winds caused by hurricanes that traveled up the East Coast of the United States. Those early experiences shaped my understanding of how important "community" is in such moments. But they also taught me how well-intentioned offerings can become an obstacle in recovering from a major disaster. I learned that some ways of helping are actually more helpful than others.

The most effective recovery occurs when the individuals, families, and communities affected by a disaster play an integral role in determining their own recovery process. Families and communities need to know which resources are available to them and which will be the best tools for recovery. Government assistance for disaster survivors abounds, but accessing it is often a challenging, lengthy, and frustrating experience. Community support, especially through faith-based organizations, is often the most helpful factor in supporting individuals and families who are journeying to recovery.

As my own family learned years ago, and which has been reinforced to me in my professional experience coordinating emergency response and disaster programs, the first step is to "expect the unexpected." If and when a disaster occurs, those who are affected by it are best-served when faith communities are well-informed and prepared to function as advocates, spiritual care givers, donors, and support networks.

During my family's brush with disaster, our home had flooded and a group from a local church spent four days helping us "mud out" and power-wash the lower level of our home. I'll never forget my father's heartfelt words to the volunteers: "I can't tell you how much your help has meant to us. This felt like an impossible job."

What could be more important than helping someone accomplish what feels discouragingly impossible? As faith-based communities, that is our calling in times of disaster. Through the guidance and expertise offered in this book, I invite you to be better prepared to care for those affected by disaster.

Donna J. Derr
Director, Development and Humanitarian Assistance
Church World Service

Preface

Disasters: the "expected" unexpected. But how might we expect what is always, necessarily, and unfortunately unexpected? Whether a freak storm or a school shooting, disasters surprise us. They shock us. Almost without exception, they catch us off guard, unaware, unsuspecting, and unequipped. Even the most earnest attempts by experts—in the fields of meteorology, environmental science, economics, sociology, and international relations—to predict potential crises do not safeguard us from the crises occurring, of course. Nor do these predictions change our expectations about what could happen. There is no way around it: disasters, by nature, are simply unexpected. For most of us in the North American context, the possibility of disaster striking—either natural or human-caused—is not on our day-to-day radar screens.

Expecting and preparing are two vastly different notions, however. While we know, intellectually, to expect disasters, we rarely do. Yet they still occur, and they feel unexpected to us. But we *can* prepare for disasters. We cannot necessarily prevent them, but we can prepare for them. We can act proactively to inform, organize, and equip ourselves for when an emergency will inevitably take place. Thus, this resource.

After eight intensive years on the staff of the Christian Church (Disciples of Christ)'s relief and development ministry, I have learned not only to expect the unexpected, but, more importantly, to prepare for it. I also quickly learned that one of my primary tasks is to help others prepare for the expected unexpected. I was to begin my new position with Week of Compassion—the relief, refugee, and development mission fund—on September 1, 2005. I actually began on August 29—in the throes of Hurricane Katrina. There was no time to waste—not even the three days between the 29th and the 1st. Too much work needed to be done: too many pastors to call, congregations to visit, funds to raise, and cleanup to begin. Eventually there would be far too many houses to gut out, mold to scrub, debris to clear, church members to console, families to comfort, solidarity grants to send, ecumenical meetings to coordinate, long-term recovery groups to organize, and stories to tell. There would be stories of sadness and suffering, as well as stories of faith and fortitude.

They would be stories of disaster and all that encompasses it—both the hardship and the hope.

The help we offer one another during times of disaster enables us to handle the hardship and provides us with hope to hold on for the future. What is most important is understanding *how* to help.

All disasters, by definition, are local. They are contextual. They happen in a certain place, at a specific time, and are always unique and different from any other disaster that has ever occurred. Yet there are commonalities present in all catastrophes, and, thus, common ways to respond. So what are those best practices? When is it most useful to offer assistance? What kinds of assistance are most needed? Who is best suited to offer that assistance? Because all disasters are indeed local, what is the role, if any, of outside assistance? How appropriate are material donations such as food, clothing, and other items? When, if ever, is the optimal time for unskilled volunteers to reach out during a disaster? Most pointedly for the purposes of this project, how might congregations and other faith communities stock their disaster response toolboxes? How are faith communities uniquely positioned to respond to individuals and communities post-disaster? What are the tools most appropriate and distinctive among congregations to enable them to offer both help and hope?

As the world witnesses the devastating, and, in many cases, irreversible, effects of climate change, it has become increasingly clear that the sheer number of natural (or so-called "natural") disasters is on the rise. Tornadoes are touching down in France for the first time in history. Airplane turbulence is consistently stronger, and flights are crossing anything but "friendly" skies. Record snowfalls in areas of the U.S. Midwest are ushering in summer. Hurricanes such as Sandy caught everyone in Atlantic City, across the Jersey Shore, and through New York City to Staten Island completely by surprise, also affecting the Caribbean countries and 24 states from Florida to Maine and even into Canada. This hurricane spawned the phrase, "super-storm"—a fitting name in a time when severe weather is becoming the norm. While political debates concerning the causes of climate change continue, what is certain is that the disasters are frequent, more destructive, and demand a more sophisticated and premeditated response.

This book aims to equip congregations with the tools necessary to respond to natural disasters, and to offer guidance to faith communities as they cope with other human-caused crises. Just as severe weather and changing weather patterns seem to be causing more natural disasters, the world's ever-changing and struggling economies, political instability, ethnic strife, and increasing demands for natural resources also lead to tremendous human need and suffering. Hunger, poverty, displacement, disease, violent conflict, and war are plaguing humanity. For many Americans, news of yet another mass shooting no longer seems surprising. It no longer feels safe to run a marathon, or go to the cinema to see a movie, or send your child to school—even in higher income and seemingly immune communities.

Regardless of the type, each disaster, by definition, causes harm. Each disaster affects the well-being of Creation. Peoples' lives are impacted. Changed. In some tragic cases, lost. In all cases, disasters merit a response.

Consider this book your disaster response toolbox. A nuanced look at all aspects of any emergency response, this resource offers practical tips for any individual, group, layperson, ordained clergy, youth, or mature adult to become better informed and equipped to react during and after disaster strikes. All the practical tips and tools inside these pages have been applied. They have been tested and can be trusted—offered to you, the reader, as part of the contributors' lived experiences. Insight is offered from theological, pastoral, spiritual, psychosocial, psychological, liturgical, and ecological perspectives. Experts in spiritual and emotional care, trauma healing, children's psychology, congregational life, pastoral care—and in the disaster, emergency response, and humanitarian sector—offer vital information for how anyone can not only respond to a disaster but also, and just as importantly, prepare for a disaster.

With this hope of preparedness, we commend these pages of practical and powerful information, insights, and inspiration. None of the contributors to this book ever expected to experience a disaster, let alone be so changed by it that they would eventually offer tips on how to prepare and respond. The question is not, "Will a disaster strike my community?" It is, rather, "When disaster strikes my community and affects my life, how might I be best prepared to respond to it?"

The answers to that very question lie inside. Prepare to expect the unexpected; it is holy work.

Amy Gopp
June 26, 2013

Amy Gopp is director of member relations and pastoral care for Church World Service. An ordained pastor in the Christian Church (Disciples of Christ), she formerly served as executive director of Week of Compassion.

The Expected Unexpected

Prepare to Be Changed

What Happens to a Disaster-Affected Congregation

JILL CAMERON MICHEL

Early on the morning of August 6, 2012, a fire burned west of Joplin, Missouri. Even though the fire department responded quickly, all that remained as the sun rose that morning was the smoldering remains of a building—the building that housed the Islamic Society of Joplin.

In the days that followed the fire, something amazing happened in Joplin. People came together in support of our Muslim friends and neighbors. Several faith communities whose leaders had worked with the local imam (the Islamic faith leader) in the past hosted an Iftar dinner (it happened to be the holy month of Ramadan) at the local Episcopal Church and invited the Muslim believers to hold prayers in the parlor. A student at the local Bible college started planning a community event of support. On the Sunday after the fire, many of us came together to place a full page ad in the local newspaper that read, "Deeply saddened by recent events, the faith communities of the Joplin area stand by our neighbors from the Islamic Society in their time of tragedy. We believe that 'Love thy Neighbor' has no restrictions." Listed on that ad were over one hundred names, primarily of pastors and faith communities: Roman Catholic and mainline Protestant, Jewish, Baha'i, Pentecostal and others.

Jill Cameron Michel is an ordained minister in the Christian Church (Disciples of Christ) who has served congregations in Missouri, Kentucky, and Kansas. A decade into her ministry at South Joplin Christian Church in Joplin, Missouri, she had the challenge and privilege of pastoring that community in the aftermath of Joplin's May 2011 tornado.

Looking at the list of signatures on this statement, I was aware that not only did support cross lines of faith, but even among the Christian partners (which were the majority) were those whose differences kept them from coming to the communion table together and whose understandings would make them hard-pressed to put their names on a single statement about Jesus.

As I surveyed the names, I couldn't help but be aware that this list was likely much different than it would have been just fifteen months earlier.

* * * * *

On May 22, 2011, an EF-5 tornado tore through Joplin. When people emerged from the rubble, or when they went into the tornado-devastated path searching for a family member or wanting to help someone in need, the lines of division that usually play a role in how we relate had all but disappeared. When shouting the name of a person not yet found, no one asked if that person was black or white; no one asked if they were Christian, Jewish, Muslim, or atheist. Politics and economics did not matter when combing through rubble. In the aftermath of that tornado we learned something about what really makes a community.

Changes of heart are worthy of celebration. However, these are not the only changes that occur in the face of disaster. We also learned how to prepare for that which we hope never happens. We learned is that, in some ways, we were more prepared than we realized. In other ways, we could have been better prepared. Today we know that the more prepared we are—whether or not we ever face disaster again—the better our ministry, even our routine and expected ministry, will be.

* * * * *

5:41 p.m. is the official time the tornado hit Joplin. Not long after that, I learned that a particular family's home had been directly in its path. As the evening grew later and I managed to make it into town, the scope of damage began to set in. Even a week later, after long days trying to connect with congregation members, I was still discovering damaged neighborhoods that I had not even known that I needed to be concerned about. Within a congregation that averages fewer than one hundred people on Sunday mornings, we had more than fifteen families who lost their homes, and countless others who experienced varying degrees of damage. With homes destroyed, telephone lines out, and fewer cell towers standing, locating people was difficult. Weeks later, we were still searching for one man from our congregation. For those who lost their homes, apartments were few and far between. Even finding someone who could suggest available housing proved to be difficult.

Months later, as people settled into new homes and made plans for the future, and as damaged homes were repaired; we started to ask our members for information for the church directory: address, phone number, birth date, and e-mail address. We also added some new questions:

Who is your local emergency contact person?

Who is your out-of-town emergency contact person?

Where would you go in case of emergency?

These questions not only prepare us for natural disasters, but will also prove helpful in health crises and other unforeseen events. See a sample Family Information Form available for download on the Help & Hope page of chalicepress.com.

*   *   *   *   *

Not only were families in our church directly impacted, but our church building also sustained damage. Although not in the direct path of the tornado, it stood close enough to the funnel's winds to fall victim to their force. The roof was torn off and windows were broken out. For two days, rain poured into the building. The nearly completed task of a recent capital campaign had to be restarted and an additional 50 percent of the interior had to be gutted.

This presented several problems for our congregation and others like us. First, where would we meet? Clearly, meeting in our building was not possible. However, our sister congregation across town welcomed us without question. The pastor of that congregation pulled a table into her office to give me my own desk. Worship times were negotiated, Sunday school space was shared. Even though our congregations hadn't had a significant relationship prior to the tornado (other than being part of the same denomination), the arrangement worked easily, because of our historical connection and simply because of compassion.

So we had a place to meet. But no matter how good the hospitality was, we didn't want to be there forever. Again, preparation was important. Although none of us had expected a tornado, we had begun in recent years to take seriously the stewardship of our building. A few years earlier we had conducted an assessment of our facility and crafted a long-range plan for building improvements. Our recent capital campaign was the first in a plan that included three capital campaigns over ten to fifteen years. Thus, when it rained in our sanctuary, we were not without a plan. The tornado did not force us to ask for the first time with what we would replace our nearly forty-year-old blue carpet. It was not the first occasion for conversation about improving our worship or education space.

When the time came to begin putting the church back together, we were *ready*. We did not have to spend months wondering or dreaming about what that might look like. We did not have to spend time—which was in high demand in a community in the midst of recovery—meeting to determine what we could and could not change. We also did not find ourselves making decisions out of fear or desperation or sheer exhaustion. We had a plan in place. Yes, there were still decisions to be made, but, for the most part, those decisions could be entrusted to a small group of people.

Another important piece of this equation was insurance. If you are a property chair or a trustee of a church or even, like me, the pastor, read your insurance policy. Know your coverage. Do not make the mistake of skimping on insurance as a cost-cutting measure because you hope a disaster might never happen to you. It might have never happened to us— but it did. We were fortunate to have excellent coverage from an excellent company specializing in insuring churches.

Because we had excellent coverage, we knew how we would put our church back together, and we were able to create a more welcoming space that was better suited to the ministries to which we are called.

And, in the midst of many physical concerns—about both people and property—spiritual concerns are a constant. I realized that the way we talk about God on usual days makes a difference in how we are able to help people understand God through the days that are unexpectedly difficult. When I have talked about my understanding of God, I have often wondered if my theology would stand up to my tragedy. And I am grateful for each day that I do not really need the answer to that question. I am also aware that the question has to be asked. For, when the winds blow and carry away all evidence of people's history; when waters rise and drown out the memories; when unexpected tragedy occurs, people need to know the love and comfort of God.

In the face of disaster, tremendous and unavoidable changes occur. Some, such as learning that we are all more alike than different, are simply gifts. Others, such as locating people, finding temporary space, remodeling or rebuilding buildings, and developing a theology that works in tragedy, are things for which we can prepare. Taking the time to prepare, even if a disaster never strikes, will serve your congregation— and your entire community—well.

QUESTIONS _____

1. Where would you go in case of disaster? Who knows your plan?

2. What intentional communication within your church ensures that people share these plans? If this is not happening, what can you do to help it happen?

3. When was the last time your congregation did a serious assessment of its facilities? Do you have a long-range building plan? What would it take to create a plan if suddenly you had to remodel or rebuild your facility?

4. When was the last time you congregation's insurance policy was reviewed? Is it sufficient? Does someone in your congregation know the details of your policy well enough to negotiate a fair settlement?

5. How do you understand God's role in world crises? How do you talk about that? Is your understanding helpful both when things are going well and when disaster strikes?

Hurricanes and Lilies

Glimpses of God When Disaster Strikes

JOSÉ F. MORALES JR.

"...the earth was without shape or form, it was dark over the deep sea, and God's wind swept over the waters... God said, 'Let the earth grow plant life...'"

GENESIS 1:2, 11A (CEB)

"There are hurricanes in the world as well as lilies."

ABRAHAM JOSHUA HESCHEL[1]

Can awful, life-robbing disasters and a good, life-giving God coexist?

This is the perennial question that haunts the faithful. To date, no satisfactory answer has been given. No fulfilling answer for the displaced thousands who to this day (still!) have not returned home to New Orleans after Katrina. No real resolution for the mother holding her child on the sidewalk, both now homeless because of a tornado that ripped through their town. No compelling justification given to the village starving because the soil has become barren due to drought. To the detached theologian or the well-to-do families living in prosperous lands, there may

José F. Morales Jr. is the executive regional minister of the Central Rocky Mountain Region of the Christian Church (Disciples of Christ). Previously he served as associate pastor of Iglesia del Pueblo-Hope Center (Disciples of Christ) in Hammond, Indiana, during which he was a community organizer and adjunct professor at McCormick Theological Seminary in Chicago. In his brief time as regional minister, the region he serves has been afflicted by both natural and human-caused disasters, included rampant wildfires and mass shootings.

be satisfying "biblical" answers, but not to those who have encountered disastrous death at a personal, intimate level.

The summer of 2012 was a long one for me and for the beloved Church I serve. Wildfires devoured tons of acreage along the front range of the Rockies, destroying homes, devastating the ecosystem, and shocking the state of Colorado. And after a series of wildfires that left firefighters depleted and communities of care with compassion fatigue, the unthinkable happened. In July of that year, a masked man killed or injured dozens in a packed movie theater in Aurora, Colorado. This man didn't pick and choose; he didn't select by age, race, gender, or class. He shot everyone in sight indiscriminately. The next morning, as public servants and religious communities sought to respond to the victims and to the community at large, the unspoken question was heard loud and clear: "Where was God in all this?"

In response to this unthinkable horror, I composed and sent a pastoral letter to all the congregations in the Central Rocky Mountain Region of my denomination:

July 20, 2012

Psalm 88:1–6, 9–13 (CEB)—

> LORD, *God of my salvation,*
>> *by day I cry out,*
>> *even at night, before you—*
>> *let my prayer reach you!*
> *Turn your ear to my outcry*
>> *because my whole being is filled with distress;*
>> *my life is at the very brink of hell.*
> *I am considered as one of those plummeting into the pit.*
>> *I am like those who are beyond help,*
>> *drifting among the dead*
>> *lying in the grave, like dead bodies—*
>> *those you don't remember anymore,*
>> *those who are cut off from your power...*
> *My eyes are tired of looking at my suffering*
>> *I've been calling out to you every day,* LORD—
>> *I've had my hands outstretched to you!*
> *Do you work wonders for the dead?*
>> *Do ghosts rise up and give you thanks?*
> *Is your faithful love proclaimed in the grave,*
>> *your faithfulness in the underworld?*
> *Are your wonders known in the land of darkness,*
>> *your righteousness in the land of oblivion?*

> *But I cry out to you, LORD!*
> *My prayer meets you first thing in the morning!*

Early this morning, while many slept safely in their homes, a gunman opened fire at the Century 16 Theater in Aurora, Colorado, killing 12 (most current count), and injuring dozens more. As we can imagine, this has stunned our human family in Aurora, Denver Metro, and beyond. Many of those killed and wounded in this atrocity were young; some were little children. This comes on the heels of the ravaging wildfires in our Region. So this goes without saying: it has been a long summer for us.

In these tragic moments, there are no set of doctrines, no quick-answer Bible verses that can calm our fears, satiate our anger, dispel our doubts, or make sense of the darkness at work in the world. (The shadows of the Columbine massacre still linger over us.) The unsettling "why" questions become the sole substance of our thoughts and prayers: Why us? Why them and not us? Why now? Why here? Why, God? Why?

While there are no quick answers in the Bible, the Bible nonetheless makes space, and even sanctions, our anger, doubts, fears, and laments.

> *"...my life is at the very brink of hell.*
> *I am considered as one of those plummeting into the pit.*
> *I am like those who are beyond help,*
> *drifting among the dead*
> *lying in the grave, like dead bodies..."*

In responding to this massacre, I encourage us, as the Body of Christ, to begin here: with honest lament, with raw prayer.

> *"LORD, God of my salvation,*
> *by day I cry out,*
> *even at night, before you—*
> *let my prayer reach you!*
> *Turn your ear to my outcry*
> *because my whole being is filled with distress..."*

Our first task as the Church is to begin with this raw prayer. For, in moments like these, raw prayer is faithful prayer.

Then our raw prayer will fund our incarnational presence and faithful action. Though we don't have answers, we do have power—power to serve, to care, to heal. I invite the whole Region to offer compassion and support to those affected in any way that is helpful and not intrusive. We have four Disciples congregations in Aurora, which are closest to the tragedy: New Covenant Christian Church, Tabernáculo de Restauración, First Christian Church, and Fireside Christian Church. I invite the whole Region to reach out to our sister congregations in Aurora and partner with them as they respond to their community. Your Region is ready to support, as is Week of Compassion, the disaster response fund of our General Church.

The psalmist, in his honest prayer, asks,

"Is your faithful love proclaimed in the grave,
    your faithfulness in the underworld?
Are your wonders known in the land of darkness,
    your righteousness in the land of oblivion?"

Ultimately, we the Church can answer the psalmist's question. By standing with the victims and their families, by praying for police, firefighters, nurses, and doctors on the ground, by offering Christ's presence in the midst of pain, suffering, and death, we the Church can indeed proclaim God's faithful love, God's faithfulness, and God's wonder "in the land of darkness."

Central Rocky Mountain Region, amidst this catastrophe, we can be Church, we can be the very presence of the Crucified and Risen Christ. May it be so!

With sorrow in my heart and tears in my eyes,

José F. Morales, Jr.
Executive Regional Minister

At such times of crisis and horrific human-caused disaster, while there are never answers to all our questions, sometimes the most comforting words are those that also reveal your own sadness and vulnerability.

And the question remains: Can awful, life-robbing disasters and a good, life-giving God coexist? The Christian faith, and the Jewish tradition from which it emerged, have wrestled with this irreconcilable question of theodicy since the beginning. How can suffering and evil coexist with an all-knowing, all-powerful, and all-loving God? Answers to the theodicy problem have been suggested by theologians and atheists, nuns and lawyers, artists and farmers. And while the answers are manifold, most traditional answers fall under two umbrella themes: "It's God's Will" and the Rational Negotiation approach. Both offer flawed views of creation and God, and are incapable of fueling our compassionate presence and service.

The "God's Will" argument simply states that God is all-powerful and either "permitted" or outright orchestrated the disaster, natural or human-caused, to get the attention of the wicked and to call them (us?) to repentance. Yet this appeal to divine will has too many holes in it, and raises more questions than answers. The most disturbing question it raises is this: If God is punishing the wicked, why do innocent people (like infants) die while the "wicked" elsewhere remain and even prosper? (See Ps. 73 and Jer. 12:1.) Beyond the holes in this argument, this approach tends to lead to human apathy and inaction. It also lacks pastoral recourse to aid the victims in their suffering; if anything, it turns these victims of the disaster into the perpetrators or, even worse, into the very victims of God.

The Rational Negotiation approach is problematic because it turns something as emotional and visceral as the trauma of natural disasters into a removed and detached academic exercise. Put succinctly, this approach seeks to *rationalize* the disaster in hopes of explaining the "whys" of the circumstance. Sometimes, we rationalize, "If we had been there, we could've stop it!" Or, "It was the sin in my life or in that city that caused the disaster!" Yet, rationalizing leaves us with way more questions than answers; and the new questions are worthless because they depend on blame and shame, or on speculation.

The historic way that the problem of theodicy has been handled is a prime example of the Rational Negotiation approach. Theologians throughout the centuries have sought to rationalize—make sense of—how God and disaster can coexist. The basic formula is this:

It is said that God is all-powerful, all-knowing, and all-loving.
But, since there's suffering in the world, God cannot be all three.
Therefore, one of the three attributes of God has to go:

Either God is all-powerful and all-knowing, but not all-loving; and is a cruel or evil Being for letting bad things happen.

Or God is all-powerful and all-loving, but not all-knowing; and is unable to foresee disasters from happening.

Or God is all-knowing and all-loving, but not all-powerful; and simply cannot overcome the power of evil or stop disasters.

This approach is purely rational, seeking to intellectually understand a good God in a world full of bad things.

Yet the Bible *never* addresses disaster in rational ways. After all, holding a dead child in one's arms is neither detached nor removed; nor is it experienced intellectually. And one cannot rationalize the feelings of insecurity, doubt, fear, and anger that come with tragedy and death. So, while we sit comfortably at abundant tables discussing God's goodness, knowledge, and power, the village ravaged by drought fears that they will not have enough crops come harvest time. Suffering from disaster is always raw and personal, deeply felt and experienced. Walter Brueggemann rightly points out that the Bible, in wrestling with the issue of human suffering, "refuses a rational, logical resolution, opting instead for a relational understanding of God, world, and the community of faith."[2] As such, our way of making sense theologically of natural disasters must likewise be relational, emotive, and—dare I say it—raw.

In developing a biblically rooted theology of disaster, we are challenged to rethink, in light of a world full of suffering, how we view both creation and God as Creator. These new perspectives can then inform how we as a people of faith offer presence and ministry in those places where suffering abounds.

Creation

Terence Fretheim states, "God created the world good, not perfect."[3]
He goes on to say, "Genesis does not present the creation as a
finished product wrapped up with a big red bow and handed
over to the creatures to keep it exactly as originally created."[4]
An important feature of Genesis 1 to highlight in this regard is found
in verse 2. According to this first creation story, the world was ordered
out of chaos—that is, out of the formless and shapeless "dark over the
deep sea." Yet, interestingly, by the end of the sequence, there is not a
definitive statement that assures us that this "dark of the deep sea" has
been eradicated completely from the universe. Hence Genesis 1 seems to
suggest that this chaos, though tamed and restricted, is still present in the
world. Brueggemann writes, "...chaos is on the loose, pushing against the
boundaries of creation."[5]

A faithful theology of disaster begins here, with an affirmation that
we live in an unfinished world, in unfinished bodies, where disasters are an
unfortunate and inevitable byproduct of said incompleteness, and that in
this continually woven fabric of creation, there are catastrophic wrinkles,
tears, and frayed edges. In this beautiful yet delicate world, chaos "was
there, is always there and is always being tamed" by God.[6]

When we affirm this harsh yet profound truth about creation, we are
moved to become good stewards of the tender life in this tender world.
We grow to appreciate the miracle of this life-sustaining world, a world
in which water produces both lilies and hurricanes.

God as Creator

While the Rational Negotiation and "God's Will" arguments seek
to understand or accept God's power, an authentic theology of disaster
tries to grasp and enter into God's *passion*. After all, as stated earlier,
encounters with natural catastrophe are not an intellectual endeavor, but
an emotional, bodily experience. The Bible, like life itself, handles disaster
in similar ways.

The Bible says many things about God's relation to suffering,
calamity, and strife—at times, contradictory things. Yet the scriptural
witness is vividly clear about one thing: God suffers with us in our
suffering. Unlike Aristotle's god who is the "Unmoved Mover,"[7]
the God of Israel, who became flesh in Jesus Christ, is the Most Moved
Mover. God's heart is fully invested in creation's well-being, and absolutely
devastated by its suffering. When God calls Moses to lead the Hebrews
out of slavery in Egypt, God speaks from the heart, "I've clearly seen my
people oppressed in Egypt. *I've heard their cry* of injustice because of their
slave masters. *I know about their pain*" (Ex. 3:7, CEB, emphasis added). St.

Paul declares that the Spirit knows our pain, and "deeply groans" with a groaning creation. (See Rom. 8:19–26.)

For Christians, the cross is the place where God chose to be fully present in human suffering. There, God suffered completely *with* us. Now, this may seem as if God is impotent; but, in actuality, the opposite is true. God's omnipotence is expressed not in God's dominance over us but in God's love for us—a love that is "limitless in its patience and infinite in its forbearance."[8] As theologian Jürgen Moltmann puts it, "If God were incapable of suffering in the fullest sense, then He would be incapable of loving."[9] In the face of natural disasters, we put our trust in a "crucified God,"[10] in Christ who suffers with us and who "sympathizes" with us (Heb. 4:15).

When we affirm this paradoxical yet profound truth about God, we are moved to be likewise engaged—heart and all—in the suffering of others. To have faith in the Most Moved Mover means that we too are moved to suffer with those who suffer. That's what *compassion* literally means: to suffer *(-passion)* with *(com-)*. And our compassionate solidarity begins with something we in the West are not comfortable with: namely, prayers of lament. Lament is a richly biblical practice of *public*, anguished prayer to God in the face of trial and tribulation. But, in our day and age, we are discouraged from being "too emotional" in the presence of others. Instead, when tears uncontrollably run down our cheeks, we are told, "Get it together!" and, "You're making a scene!"

Yet this is where we must begin when disaster strikes: with raw, honest prayer to God, calling God to respond, to heal, to tame the chaos and bring back the lilies. We pray this way, not because of lack of faith, but because of deep faith—deep faith in a loving God who hears our cries. We lament to a God who laments with us. And these laments of ours will in turn fuel our compassionate presence and action in the world. It is out of our cries for "wholeness in a fragmented world"[11] that our ministry springs forth.

In short, our theology of disaster is incomplete without a robust spirituality of lament and the compassionate, "suffer-with" action that grows from it. So, let's begin here...

> Let's wrestle with God; let's lament; let's argue with God on the side of human dignity and human life. Let's rail against natural destruction and devastation; let's rail against death...with great hope and faith that in the end God, too, is on the side...[of life].[12]

Whether in hurricanes or lilies, God is always—always—with us.

QUESTIONS _____

1. How do you understand God's role in the midst of suffering? Since

disaster exists, is God lacking in love, knowledge, or power? Or is there a way to affirm all three attributes in light of a world full of suffering?

2. Genesis 1 calls creation and humans "good." Yet, Morales argues that creation is good, yet incomplete. Do you agree with his argument? Why or why not?

3. The Book of Lamentations was written during crisis and tragedy. The book portrays God as harsh and, at times, cruel. Read Lamentations 3:1–27. Discuss the portrait of God depicted there. What are your thoughts and feelings about this image of God?

4. Think about an encounter you or a loved one has had with tragedy or disaster. Write a lament psalm to God. (For examples, read Ps. 13; 22.)

3

Where Your Treasure Is

Stewardship and Disaster Response

JOHNNY WRAY

When disaster strikes and our television and computer screens are filled with those powerful and poignant images of people whose homes have been destroyed by flood or wildfire, whose lives have been ravaged by famine or war, whose communities have been devastated by earthquake or tornado—our hearts are moved and we want to respond. And rightly so. But with so many organizations, private and public, religious and secular, making their appeals for our monetary and material donations, how does one indeed respond rightly, compassionately, and faithfully? How can we best ensure that our gifts are used wisely and well to meet the needs of those most affected by the disaster? How can we preclude our responses from becoming "a disaster within a disaster?"

These questions became overwhelmingly apparent to me in the aftermath of the very first disaster I was called to respond to as Director of Week of Compassion for the Christian Church (Disciples of Christ). The year was 1992 and Hurricane Andrew had devastated much of southern Florida. My initial trip to the area was to visit our affected congregations and members and to see the relief and recovery work of our local partners.

The personal stories of loss and the broader scenes of destruction were deeply affecting. The good work of our on-the-ground partners was equally encouraging. What was distressing was to learn how unneeded

Johnny Wray is resource development associate of Week of Compassion presently, and previously directed the ministry from 1992 to 2008. During that time he worked closely with partners to coordinate responses to disasters at home and abroad. He and his wife Deb live, work, and enjoy life on their small farm in Mississippi.

donations proved to be not only inconvenient but actually a hindrance to the work of those partners: the outside donations of used clothing, for example. With little need for used clothing and no place to store these donations, it was not uncommon for piles of clothes to join the debris on the way to the growing landfill outside Miami.

A few years later, I was again visiting congregations and local partners in Oklahoma City, this time in response to a devastating tornado that had swept through the city. There were more moving stories of loss, images of destruction, and examples of good work by our partners—but also more accounts of unhelpful responses. One local congregation serving as an emergency distribution center had received a phone call from a church in another state that intended to—that very day—send a tractor trailer load of refrigerators, washing machines, ovens, beds and other household items. The local pastor said, "Thanks, but you'll have to wait. What we actually need are cleaning supplies, nonperishable food, vouchers for clothes and medicines." In other words, what they really needed were monetary donations so that they, themselves, could determine and purchase what their people most needed at that time. But the pastor on the other line was incredulous and insistent, "We've got the truck loaded, we're ready to pull out right now." Once again the local pastor pleaded, "Thank you. But please understand. We have no place to store them. Even more, the folks who will need them no longer have homes in which to put them!"

Then there was the trip to Central America in the aftermath of Hurricane Mitch, one of the deadliest, costliest, and most destructive disasters in the Western Hemisphere during the twentieth century. A local Honduran faith-based organization, anticipating the outpouring of relief supplies and rebuilding materials from its international network of partners, had secured a second warehouse, which was rapidly filling. The staff was worried that additional (and costly) space might be needed to store donated materials that were not particularly needed or helpful. "What might that be?" I inquired. I was shown boxes of used clothing—a good bit of it heavy, winter clothing sized for much larger North Americans. Honduran winters are rainy but not cold. I saw pallets piled high with boxes and boxes of canned foods, vegetables and fruits of all kinds. "What could possibly be a problem with that?" I asked. I learned people in the countryside eat primarily rice and beans; "They don't know about canned mushrooms and asparagus and fruit cocktail. But, besides, have you ever tried to open a can of tomatoes with a machete?" Apparently, can openers are not a typical item in the Honduran household.

Sometimes even our most well-intentioned efforts produce unintended and unhelpful results.

This is why stewardship is such an integral part of our compassionate response to disasters. As people of faith, we are called to be both generous and judicious with the resources that have been entrusted to us; choosing efficient and effective ways to utilize those resources embodies what it means to be compassionate.

The ancient Hebrews perceived compassion as being rooted in the bowels, in the guts. The Koine Greek word for compassion, *splagchnon*, is frequently translated in the New Testament as "bowels." A more literal translation of those passages referring to Jesus' compassion might read, "Jesus was so moved by their hunger, his own stomach ached." We typically think of compassion as coming from the heart, which is perhaps why we often confuse compassion with feelings of sympathy, pity, or sorrow. That in itself is a pity! Genuine compassion is more. It takes courage—*guts*—to be a compassionate person in the world in which we live.

If compassion is rooted in our viscera, I would suggest it is also directly connected to our minds. Like stewardship, compassion is about the conscious decisions we make with our resources. We must be gracious and generous, yes—but also thoughtful and judicious. To give proactively to denominational, faith-based, ecumenical disaster funds or other humanitarian organizations provides those responding to disaster with the means to do so immediately. To make a financial commitment to giving *before* a disaster strikes is part of the spiritual discipline of stewardship.

In Matthew's gospel, Jesus tells his hearers: "Where your treasure is, *there your heart will be also*" (Mt. 6:21, CEB, emphasis added). He did not say, "Where your heart is, your treasure will be also." Could Jesus have been encouraging us to decide carefully where to place our resources—with the assurance that our heart will follow, rather than making this choice based on how we might feel about something at the moment?

What might a compassionate response, based on solid stewardship, look like?

In the aftermath of a disaster, we regularly encourage congregations to do three things: *stay, pray, pay.*

First, *stay*. Wait. Gather as much information as possible—not just from the customary news outlets, but also from other sources, especially your denomination's disaster relief office and trusted relief organizations such as Church World Service. They often have personnel who can respond quickly, and they are able to provide invaluable information from congregations, local partners, and on-the-ground experts.

Pray. Prayer is a bond connecting us to God and others. It brings us into a deeper sense of solidarity with those most affected by disaster and it gives validity and vitality to our sense of compassion. Compassion is, after all, "suffering with." Our prayers enable us to more fully engage people in the midst of their pain. When we are not there physically, we can be there spiritually.

Pay. Most importantly, we can share our resources. Almost without exception, the most helpful way to contribute to disaster relief is through monetary donations.

We can give what is most needed and helpful to partners who are dedicated to serving those most in need. We can also channel our resources to partners who are committed to being there, not only in the initial stages of relief, but for the long road of recovery and reconstruction. Last, it is important to direct our funds to partners who are accountable, transparent, and responsible to the donors back home.

Sharing your treasure is one of the most impactful ways you can respond after a disaster. The spiritual discipline of giving *before* a disaster strikes, so that when disaster happens assistance is immediately sent, moves your compassion into action. Proactive stewardship enables needs to be immediately met, and comfort immediately offered. Faithful stewardship is one of the most powerful ways to prepare for and respond to a disaster. When you cannot be physically there in the aftermath, or when you *should not* be there lest you become a disaster within a disaster, rest assured that the stewardship of your resources is the most compassionate act you can perform. After all, it is not only *your* treasure, it is the treasure that has been entrusted to you by the great God who created you. And where that treasure is, your heart will follow!

QUESTIONS

1. Why is financial stewardship important to emphasize when responding to disasters? What is the connection between stewardship and compassion?
2. Are you (and members of your congregation) regularly receiving information and updates from your denomination's disaster relief ministry? From an ecumenical agency?
3. Does your congregation have a person or team who can convey disaster information promptly to the congregation, including the disaster's impact on sister congregations in the affected area and on your denomination's current and future responses to the disaster? Does your pastor and/or worship leader regularly include, in the congregation's common prayers, intercessions for those affected by disasters in this country and abroad?
4. Financial gifts are typically what are needed most. There are times, however, when material donations are needed and useful. Are you

and your congregation familiar with Church World Service's Gifts of the Heart Program and similar programs with other denominational partners?

5. What reasons can you give for why it is best to channel your disaster response donations through your denomination's relief office and its related partners?

4

Faith at Work around the World

A Perspective on International Disasters

CHRIS HERLINGER

The Haitian aid workers arrived with several truckloads of relief supplies—tents, blankets, and the like—at an isolated area outside the capital of Port-au-Prince, which, more than a week after the January 2010 earthquake there, still had not received any assistance.

The workers for the Lutheran World Federation had done their best to make sure the distribution went smoothly. But on the day of the distribution, any sense of order collapsed when a group of young men who were not on the list of recipients demanded some of the items and began disrupting the event. Police were called in, and although the young Haitian aid workers held their ground, the situation quickly deteriorated. People rushed the distribution center. A policewoman fired several shots; another person brandished a shotgun and people scrambled. Luckily, no one was seriously injured or hurt.

At a later debriefing, some of the Haitians wondered if the distribution should have stopped the moment it was clear there might be problems; others said that would not have been fair to those who were rightly in line and had waited patiently. Privately, some of the foreign workers wondered if the young Haitians had not been sufficiently careful or had not laid the

---

Chris Herlinger is a writer with the humanitarian agency Church World Service and is also a New York-based freelance journalist. He has authored three books on humanitarian themes and is starting work on a new book focusing on global hunger. He holds graduate degrees from Union Theological Seminary and Cambridge University.

groundwork well enough. Some suggested that the aid should have been distributed to whoever needed it.

Some of the things hinted at by the foreign workers—inexperience, a perceived lack of professionalism—are accusations sometimes leveled at those who work for faith-based humanitarian agencies. The real pros, it is sometimes assumed, are those who work for secular groups like the Red Cross and Doctors Without Borders. In Haiti, at least, those groups are seen as at the top of a humanitarian hierarchy; followed by the large faith-based groups and alliances like World Vision, Catholic Relief Services, and Caritas; in turn followed by smaller church-based groups like Church World Service; and, then, finally the smaller mom-and-pop operations, many of them evangelical Protestant.

These organizations are just a few of the hundreds of faith-based humanitarian groups out there today. In the listing of about eighty agencies that responded in Haiti and belong to a U.S.-based alliance of humanitarian groups called InterAction, about a quarter are expressly faith-based or have religious roots, and there are dozens of other smaller faith-based groups working in Haiti that do not belong to InterAction.

Christians United

I can only speak as someone who reports for Church World Service, which has ties to a wide network of other agencies—Protestant, Anglican, and Orthodox—but it often seems that some of the more common accusations against faith-based groups cut both ways. In my travels, I have met dozens of workers for faith-based groups who are committed, talented, and deeply, deeply professional. And I have met young, inexperienced staff members working for secular groups in tough, demanding places too.

In the end, most of these humanitarian organizations, faith-based or secular, have more that unites us than divides us. And the more prominent faith-based groups I have worked with—like CWS, Lutheran World Federation (LWF) and Catholic Relief Services (CRS)—are united even more closely. But our bond is not forged over the occasional need to defend ourselves from accusations or a desire to separate ourselves from secular aid groups. Rather, we are united in our shared desire to support very basic humanitarian principles, including refraining from proselytizing; and in the fact that we treat all of those affected by disasters without discrimination or favor. Greatest need is, and should be, the priority for all of us who do humanitarian work, not factors like religious affiliation, political beliefs, or ethnicity. Christian commitment undergirds what we do; and while these groups seek to touch hearts, conversion is not part of our agenda.

Yet other faith-based aid groups make no secret that they are also religious-oriented bodies that claim the right of proselytizing, or conversion, to Christianity when they do humanitarian work. This is a key difference among the Christian aid groups, and it is proof that Christianity is an enormous tent. I would not call this so much a squabble as just a very essential and different outlook on how branches of Christianity approach humanitarian work. In fact, in disaster situations like Haiti there is not a lot of interchange between humanitarian agencies of different stripes. Many non-governmental organizations I have worked with believe that the act of proselytizing is a violation of humanitarian principles. In the other corner, one evangelical I know once told me that, while she was impressed by CWS's work, she felt it was too bad we did not "take the next step" of trying to convert Muslims to Christianity. I strenuously disagreed. In the midst of disaster, members of affected communities are vulnerable in many ways—psychologically, spiritually, physically. While offering care and resources is an appropriate response, cultural and economic differences between relatively privileged aid workers and people who may have lost everything can make an act of evangelizing coercive, perhaps even exploitive. Most important, focusing on a survivor's religious identity could cause an aid worker to miss the other, more immediate issues the person faces.

An essential factor that ties all of us together—and why I still choose to work for this kind of church-based organization—is what I can only describe as something marvelously stubborn: It is the sheer durability of the Christian church. Here I am speaking of its deep roots in much of the world, and its web of relationships—from parish to town, from congregation to countryside, from hospitals to feeding centers. The Christian church has existed in the past; it is present today; and it will be present tomorrow. The Haitian workers I described worked in Haiti well before the earthquake and are still there now, doing good work three years after the disaster.

Such work is most meaningful when it is done freely and tied to the inherent dignity of our brothers and sisters rather than to the religious claims of one group or another. When I visited northern Pakistan in 2010, the work of my CWS colleagues there (both Muslim and Christian) was appreciated simply for what it was.

I well remember the afternoon I spent with seventy-two-year-old farm laborer Noor Paras, who lived in a village along the Indus River that had been damaged by floods. A quiet and dignified man, Paras knew that the Eid holiday that year was going to be a curtailed, pinched affair with little outward celebration. Yet he appreciated the food packages CWS had provided, calling them "a gift from God." It did not matter to Paras where the food came from—in emergencies there is no Islamic food or Christian food, but merely survival food.

Here is another example. In late 2011, I visited Kenya and Ethiopia on a freelance assignment for *The National Catholic Reporter*. While there, I interviewed women religious, priests, and humanitarian workers, all trying to ameliorate the effects of a terrible drought and drawn-out humanitarian crisis that had elicited little concern or attention in the United States.

One of my CWS colleagues, Sammy Mutua, told me of an increasingly prominent phenomenon: food crises in urban areas, like Nairobi, where one-time farming families had been forced to leave their land and now found themselves scrambling to find food. This scramble had become part of a difficult life in which people lost the social support they had once had, and cherished, back home.

In the midst of this kind of environment are people like Rev. Paulino Mondo of Holy Trinity Parish in the Nairobi slum of Kariobangi, and Ruth Wanjiru Mbugua, a social worker who works with the Holy Trinity community. Both were doing their best to simultaneously help feed their community (with the help of groups like CRS) and do battle against such long-standing social woes as gun violence. Outside the urban areas, Rev. Pius Kyule, a priest in the Machakos district, a rural area southeast of Nairobi, was working with CRS to implement a feeding program in an area that was feeling real pressure. Many people struggled just to keep a very basic diet of about one kilo of beans for six people on the table. This crisis of rising food prices and accompanying pressures on increasingly denuded land due to climate change were all taking a significant toll. "It's getting worse every year, and people are suffering," Kyule told me.

The Unseen End

I am asked sometimes, not surprisingly, how a loving God can allow such suffering. The question arises everywhere, not only in the Horn of Africa, but in other places where I have worked—Sudan, Indonesia, Afghanistan, Central America, and the war-torn Balkans, to name just a few.

To be honest, the question has never meant as much to me as has the privilege of seeing so many people like my Kenyan brothers and sisters simply doing their jobs, often unheralded, as they work to alleviate that suffering. Kenya was far from the worst situation I have seen, but it was serious enough, and through years of travel guided by such inspirational figures, my own sense of faith has deepened because I know they, as the church's representatives and workers, are struggling in the vineyards, are present, and will continue to be present when others have left Kenya and other places. That is where God is, I tell people. And if these humanitarian efforts are part of a web of relationships undergirded by 2,000 years of tradition and history, all the better.

Often this work is incremental, partial, and imperfect—like the aid delivery in Haiti that went awry. Aid groups need to work to minimize such failures, of course. But as someone who, with age, has become less open to "grand schemes" and is more fully aware of life's limits and snares, I believe we should not be afraid of partial or imperfect efforts, even as we strive always to do our best, our most excellent work.

We have guideposts for this. Among my colleagues at CWS, there is a popular prayer that is often attributed to one of my clerical heroes, the martyred Archbishop Oscar Romero, though it was in fact composed by Bishop Kenneth Untener of Saginaw, Michigan. It speaks about the ways in which our works are always incomplete and that "the kingdom always lies beyond us":

> We cannot do everything, and there is a sense of liberation in realizing that. This enables us to do something, and to do it very well. It may be incomplete, but it is a beginning, a step along the way, an opportunity for the Lord's grace to enter and do the rest. We may never see the end results, but that is the difference between the master builder and the worker. We are workers, not master builders; ministers, not messiahs. We are prophets of a future not our own.

Workers, indeed, imperfect as the institutions we work for. But we are present, doing our best, and, we hope, doing some good in the world, however partial.

QUESTIONS

1. The author talks about the culture of "professionalism" among humanitarian agencies. Do you think faith-based groups should be more concerned with "professionalism" or being true to the gospel? Are there instances when those priorities will be in conflict?

2. The article mentions that "Greatest need is, and should be, the priority for all of us who do humanitarian work, not factors like religious affiliation, political beliefs, or ethnicity. Christian commitment undergirds what we do; and while these groups seek to touch hearts, conversion is not part of our agenda." Do you agree with that view, or should humanitarian groups funded by the church be also concerned about "saving souls," as well as providing assistance?

3. How do you, as a person of faith, deal with the question of how a loving God can allow suffering? Does God cause natural disasters? Does human behavior play any role?

4. In the context of humanitarian work, can people "do God's work" even if they are not Christian? Could an atheist be a good humanitarian worker? Could a nonbeliever "do God's work"?

5. What might be the differences and similarities between humanitarian work in the United States and, say, Africa? How might responding to a community affected by a tornado in Oklahoma, for example, be different than responding to a tsunami in coastal Africa? How would they be similar? What strengths would each affected community bring to the response? Could they "go it alone" and recover on their own? If not, what outside help might each respective community need?

6. Rural communities in the U.S. often pride themselves on not needing outside help. Is that realistic if a community is affected by a major disaster? How can the faith community be a part of a community's rebuilding and recovery?

WHEN ANDERSON COOPER IS IN TOWN
Right after the Disaster

5

When the Phones Don't Work

TYLER WHIPKEY

Crouched inside the bathroom of the shoe store where I found shelter during the storm, I frantically sent a text message to my wife asking, "Are you okay? Where are you?" When it was safe enough to go outside, I sped to the church as fast as the debris in the road would let me. Just an hour before, an EF-5 tornado had torn through Joplin, Missouri, and I had no idea where my wife and daughter were. I had checked the house, but they weren't there. My mobile phone was practically worthless due to the crippled cellular towers. I had been trying to call for the past half hour, but I couldn't get through. All around me, I could hear sirens wailing as emergency vehicles tried to rush through the carnage to rescue those who were trapped under the rubble. Smoke filled the air from fires that had been kindled, and people began gathering on street corners and rushing to aid their neighbors. After making my way through closed roads and makeshift blockades, I ran up the steps of the church where I was serving as student pastor and quickly unlocked the door. I could hear water running into the darkened sanctuary from a hole in the roof, but I was more concerned with the landline phone in my office. I picked it up, hoping desperately for a dial tone. Silence. The building was powerless and without phone service. I was left alone in the dark, with no idea where my family was.

Tyler Whipkey is pastor of the First Christian Church (Disciples of Christ) in Laurens, Iowa. He served as the student pastor at South Joplin Christian Church (Disciples of Christ) in Joplin, Missouri, when a tornado struck that community in May of 2011. In 2012 Tyler worked with AmeriCorps and Morehead State University to oversee volunteer coordination after a tornado passed through the nearby community of West Liberty in March of that year.

Not knowing where to start looking for them, I finally received a reply saying, "We're okay." Although the voice network and landline phones had failed me, text messages had come through. Elated, I traded enough messages with my wife to find out that they had been south of the tornado, eating dinner, and were heading to her parents' house.

For the first few days after the disaster, text messages were the best way to communicate in Joplin. Text messages require fewer network resources than voice calls in order to be sent and received, making them the most dependable way to communicate with loved ones in and out of the disaster zone.

Being able to send a text message doesn't do you any good if you don't have phone numbers, though. Many churches have a membership directory with contact information, but often these exist only as a hard paper copy, or on the computer in the church office. If your building is damaged or destroyed, this information could be irretrievably lost. Luckily, I was able to get my hands on a recent directory that hadn't been damaged by water. Collecting and regularly updating members' information, along with emergency contacts and disaster plans for each household, and storing them off-site—preferably in a digital format on-line—can prove a life-saver. There are many services that allow for documents to be stored free of charge and accessed from a variety of platforms. You will find an example of a family disaster planning form in the Toolkit section of this book.

As a result of the damage to our church building from the storm, we were forced to relocate our worship services. While we could post this information on Facebook, not everyone in our congregation had access to the Internet. The best way that we found to spread the word about our worship time and location was to use an auto-dialer service. The senior pastor recorded a message that was then "auto-dialed" to all of the phone numbers that we provided to the company. While some individuals who were without phone service did not get the call, the vast majority of our members were able to access the message either from their cell phones or remote voicemail.

If an individual's home was damaged or destroyed by the tornado, we tried to find our members as best we could. This involved a couple of different tactics. First, we checked the American Red Cross website. After a disaster, the American Red Cross does an excellent job of keeping track of those affected, and publishes that information on-line. For those individuals who were not listed on the Red Cross website and unreachable by phone, we had to try to find them by first finding their homes.

I went out to look for an older church member from whom we hadn't heard. For two days after the storm, it drizzled steadily, reflecting the city's mood. I walked down streets that I had once known well and found myself completely lost. Nothing was familiar. All around me were broken homes and shops and people beginning to sift through the rubble to pull out any salvageable memories and valuables. I finally reached into my pocket and brought up the GPS app on my cell phone to figure out just where I was. After walking about six blocks, I found the church member—watching as a bulldozer cleared away a large piece of debris so he could gain entry to the home.

I walked up to him, and we embraced for a long time. His home had been destroyed, and he had nearly been taken with it. I had no words to make things better. Instead, I offered him the only thing that I had: a shoulder to cry on. He gave me the phone number and address of a friend he was staying with, and I assured him his church family would be in touch with him regularly.

The Internet Is Your Friend…*If* You Can Find It

Social networking tools were vital to my ministry after the tornado devastated our community. You may be asking yourself, "Why is social networking so important in a disaster? People don't have electricity, much less time to check Facebook!" One of the things that I failed to realize was how deeply social networking is embedded into twenty-first-century life. If you're like me, you find yourself on Facebook at least a dozen times a day to find out what's going on in the lives of those around you. When a disaster strikes, social networks becomes even more important.

On May 22, I posted "I'm okay" on my Facebook wall. That single post immediately received over twenty-three comments, and others bombarded my wall and e-mail inbox with offers of prayer and help in any way possible. For my friends who live hundreds of miles away, this was their way of reaching out and helping. They let me know that I was in their prayers and thoughts at a time when all familiarity had been torn from the landscape around me. My congregation and I were able to experience the love of friends from afar, and feel God's comfort resting upon us as we checked our computers and our cell phones in the days after the storm.

Ten months after the tornado leveled Joplin, I experienced a similar disaster in West Liberty, Kentucky. I had moved from Missouri and was serving as an AmeriCorps VISTA volunteer with Morehead State University's Center for Regional Engagement in Morehead, Kentucky. On March 2, 2012, a tornado leveled much of West Liberty's downtown area and marked a path of destruction through Morgan County. Two days later, I met with other university officials to begin formulating our response to the disaster.

We utilized all forms of social networking available to us. The university's Facebook and Twitter feeds were commandeered to distribute information, and its website became a central on-line location to find information on volunteer opportunities, news about the event, FEMA information, and a host of other things that we felt would be relevant to share.

It is important that you know your log-in information to be able to manipulate both your website and social media accounts away from your office. If you have your log-in information auto-saved on your office computer, it won't help you much if you find that you have no power at the office, or no office at all. Make sure that you store all of your user names, passwords, and other log-in information in a secure off-site location that you can readily access, such as a Google Docs document. After living through both the tornado in Joplin and then in West Liberty, I now keep this information in my wallet.

Additionally, being able to manipulate the content on your church website is important. Established websites offer an excellent platform to get information out to a lot of people without a lot of effort. While some hosting providers offer free web-based editors, other more complex sites require special web editing software to make changes while retaining the cohesive design of the site. Check with the individual(s) who regularly maintain your website and formulate a plan to make additions to the website in case of an emergency situation.

It's also important to decide what information is best communicated on-line, and what information is best communicated either via telephone or in person. In Kentucky, my primary responsibility was to coordinate the volunteers coming into the county. While we used Facebook and various websites to communicate information, such as the telephone number and operating hours for the Volunteer Reception Center, we did not communicate specific volunteer needs on-line. Information like this changes too rapidly to adequately and accurately communicate it via Facebook.

In Joplin, however, we found that Facebook was an excellent way to give people a short update on what was happening. Information such as worship service times and locations, names of individuals who were still missing, and other announcements that were important to the community were posted on both Facebook and the church website.

Unfortunately, shortly after both tornadoes that I was involved in, rumors began popping up on-line that were completely unfounded and harmful to the recovery process. For example, while I was working in Morgan County, bogus information was circulated via Facebook about a community meeting scheduled for a particular day. While such a meeting never occurred—and was not actually scheduled, people still showed up. Ripples of distrust soon spread in the midst of an already difficult time.

Social networks have the ability to spread information rapidly. However, they can also spread gossip and misinformation. While intentions are almost always good, it is easy for an individual to get one fact or another wrong, and then the misinformation spirals out of control. As a community of faith or organization responding to an emergency, it's your job to make sure that you collect and disseminate *accurate information* following a disaster. Only trust information from reliable sources, such as vetted media services or direct communications from emergency management officials. Do your best to stay up to date with local emergency management officials and other state and local agencies that are directly responding to the event. Attend community meetings and get involved with the long-term recovery process once it begins. Many law enforcement and emergency management entities are utilizing Facebook and Twitter to disseminate accurate, up-to-date information. Subscribe to those feeds and glean information from there. Contact your local authorities to make sure that you have the most accurate information to pass along, and don't be afraid to ask clarifying questions. You cannot give good information to others if you have not received it yourself.

If you do happen to come across a post with misleading or false information, you have a responsibility to counter it by setting the record straight. For example, if rumors of a bogus community meeting circulate on Facebook, a church can collect the appropriate information and post a correction, such as *"We understand that there are rumors of a meeting scheduled for Tuesday afternoon. We have consulted with the appropriate officials, and unfortunately no such meeting is scheduled at this time. We are working with the appropriate agencies to work toward an effective response, but no meeting is currently scheduled. Thank you for your patience. If you have any questions, feel free to contact us at xxx-xxx-xxxx."* You need to acknowledge the specific piece of bad information that you are addressing and do your best to correct it. When possible, name your sources (Ex: "State Emergency Management Officials informed us…, etc."). Do your best to remind everyone involved that recovering from a disaster is a long process and that everyone is working toward recovery. Always be sure to express a realistic sense of hope and, as best as you can, profile the way recovery is progressing when you counter misinformation.

One of the most important words that you can use in social media following a disaster is "wait." Many people will want to immediately rush in to help in any way they believe they can. While this is a good thing to *want* to do, in actuality it may be harmful to the overall response. In Morgan County, Kentucky, I heard tales of individuals bringing in bulldozers ready to start clearing debris in downtown West Liberty the night of the storm. While their intentions were good, they failed to realize that there were still dangers present and possibly individuals still trapped inside the buildings. Going in without a clear understanding of the situation can lead to an even bigger disaster.

While social networking tools, websites, and text messages are all excellent ways to communicate after a disaster, never underestimate the value of being present to those in need. There's simply no substitute for a hug.

QUESTIONS

1. What social networking sites do you use? What ways might they be helpful in the case of a disaster?
2. What is the most critical information you should communicate on-line?
3. Who has the ability to change content on your church's website or Facebook page? Do you have a plan for updating information in case of a disaster? See a sample Family Information Form available for download on the Help & Hope page of chalicepress.com.

6

The Role of the Media Following a Disaster

MATT HACKWORTH

The hatches were battened. Anything that hadn't been lashed down or moved inside we had deemed stout enough to take the wind. Our food pantry looked like an overstocked ship's larder. We had even prepared our eight-year-old for the eventualities of days without electricity ("That's right, you can't charge the iPad…"), and everything seemed ready. That is, until I started in on that most ancient of hurricane preparedness rituals, "The Filling of the Bathtub."

We had just moved into our home three months before Superstorm Sandy struck the East Coast. I'm an avid do-it-yourselfer, and generally love the process of getting to know a home, especially an older home that has character. Yet I wasn't ready for the slow-leaking drain that sapped what was to be our way to flush toilets for however long Sandy's effects stuck around.

I tried in vain to fix the drain in a hurry. But somewhere in between noticing the leak and throwing my locking pliers across the room in frustration, I knew I had overlooked the step in our disaster preparedness plan of making sure a system worked before I depended on it. By the time the wind grew to a roar that bent the old-growth trees lining our

Matt Hackworth is director of marketing and communication for Church World Service. A "recovering journalist," he covered stories for National Public Radio programs such as Morning Edition and All Things Considered before coming to CWS as a communication officer in the agency's emergency response program.

block, I knew our strategy had to change. Sandy was coming, regardless of my plans.

Plans change. Drains leak. Branches snap and electrical lines fall. All of it is anticipated as part of what we envision as living the disaster. Yet for many practitioners of disaster ministry, the onslaught of media in a disaster setting comes as a surprise. The drone of TV news coverage becomes easy to tune out when preparing a home like ours to face a disaster; it can be diminished even more when preparing to care for a whole community. And so, preparing for media attention (or, even how to attract it) is drowned out among the panoply of needs that practitioners of disaster ministry face before, during, and following catastrophes. Good systems of media management in long-term recovery make sure media attention is maximized and any negative effects handled in the best way possible.

Planning for disaster and what could happen ensures those we serve are afforded our best effort. Media work is integral to proper disaster preparedness. Without it, we cannot serve our brothers and sisters responsibly. When we work with the media, we can ensure that the voices of those we serve are heard and portrayed with dignity and respect. Someone must take the role of ownership in anticipating and responding to media interaction.

Disaster preparedness requires media preparedness.

Prepare to Care, Prepare to Share

The National Guard Humvee led us into the touchdown site. Out of nowhere on a Sunday night a rash of tornadoes smacked the suburbs of North Kansas City, where I was working as a reporter. The twisters obliterated a small development of upper-middle-class homes. We snaked around lawn furniture stuck in downed trees; past kitchen cabinets, beds, and other artifacts of the suburban homes now upended like matchsticks. There were around a half-dozen reporters with me, all of us after the same thing: someone who lost their home, who would give the inevitable teary interview to put the human face on their unconscionable tragedy.

It was news. I was a reporter, and I had a job to do. Airtime to fill. Listeners to clue in.

During the thirteen years I worked as a journalist, I learned that media work can be formulaic. The "never thought it could happen" interview after a disaster is an inevitable part of the equation. Newsrooms set out to find ways to tell the story at disaster's earliest dawning: the science of it, the government's management of it, the teary-eyed human face of it, and everything in between. The days following the disaster event are filled with stories of "recovery," until fatigue and malaise force the event from the news cycle.

The perception long-held in disaster ministry is that when the cameras turn elsewhere, our job is just getting started. In reality, our job in long-term recovery should start well before the disaster event. It's critical to work in partnership with social service agencies, other faith communities, government and voluntary organizations, and any other group that touches vulnerable communities—not only to ensure that cases of need are managed and resources are leveraged, but to also lay the groundwork of good media preparedness.

In the days following the disaster, our connections can help make sure that pockets of overlooked need are afforded media attention. The reporter's need for the human face is a natural opportunity to promote the work of long-term recovery. Planning for who will handle this kind of work, and under what circumstances putting forward a human face in a vulnerable community will be brought to bear, helps ensure that the communities we serve are presented with dignity and respect instead of spectacle and pity.

The long-term recovery group's charge is to partner with communities, affording them full participation in the achievement of finding a new "normal" following disaster. While finding an underserved community and exposing it to the media's gaze may seem like it's playing into media's predisposition for drama, it affords a chance to control the story rather than merely responding to it. By being in front of the story, leading reporters to affected communities, caring communities help to ensure the message conveyed is one of partnership, dignity, and capacity.

Who Does What, When, Where, Why and How

Just as every affected community has capacity to recover, so too does the long-term recovery group have ability to handle media. Mike Wallace or the White House Press Secretary may not be at the table. But there are always those with connections, or even a mere willingness to help handle media. It's critical to identify who that person may be in "peacetime." Discuss what happens when a disaster strikes. Or when a reporter calls. Bring it up during the discussion of the mechanics of just how the group will function.

It's best that one person handles media for the group. Otherwise, reporters can get confused, competing interests can overtake good stories, and nothing will get covered.

So much of this is simply about helping the reporter do the job. Newsrooms are shrinking. Newspapers alone cut nearly a third of the medium's overall workforce since 2001, according to the Pew Center's

"State of the News Media 2013 Report." Yet, even as fewer people work in newsrooms, the demand for content is growing—which means the group that best helps a reporter find stories or voices within a story is most likely to get coverage. It's important to respond to inquiries quickly, and to follow through. If you have an idea, it's best to call earlier in the day than later. And, don't be afraid to pitch your idea to individual reporters in multiple ways: e-mail, telephone call; even Twitter handles are a growing way of steering reporters to the story.

What's the Story?

In the days following disaster, communication among those at the table is critical. A good starting point is to discern pockets of need. For example, listen for communities affected that may not be getting the resources they need. Often, these are communities labeled by society based on their differences: "the disabled," "minorities," "undocumented..." The list is long. The communities faith-based agencies serve rarely are afforded a positive voice in the modern media environment. Part of accompanying these groups on the journey to recovery is empowering them to tell their stories.

A group at the table that works most closely with a community of need should help to identify a person (or persons) from within that community who would be willing to tell their story in the media, without pressure or promise of reciprocity. True, it creates the danger of public support for an individual rather than the community. However, there is no better way to make use of the news cycle to promote recovery in the much longer term. Long-term recovery in itself is not a "sexy" story, but a woman who cannot leave her home to reach a feeding station because a flood has washed away her wheelchair ramp will get people's attention. It's our job to help the reporter learn of it, and to put it into perspective: How many other persons with limitations have been overlooked? That's why it is critical to observe pockets of need following disaster, as opposed to individual stories unique to one family. The groups at your table know the areas of need best, and can help reporters to see that wider need through one family's story.

When the Phone Rings

The odds and ends of mapping out how to route cases, donations, volunteers, and other pieces of the long-term recovery puzzle too often lack the answer to a basic question: What happens when reporters call?

On the practical side it's best to make sure everyone in your group knows one person is the primary contact for media. This makes the reporter's work easier and keeps messaging clean and simple. It's OK for this media contact not to have all the answers, or to help the reporter talk to the person at the table best equipped to answer an inquiry. But it should start with one person who answers initially.

Any reporter will want to speak with a single person or family that represents the issue they're trying to cover. Start with case managers. They grow to know their clients quite well. Don't be afraid to ask case managers in meetings for clients who they think would be good to represent the work of long-term recovery. It's a lot easier to have those discussions and seek the client's permission *before* a reporter calls than to wait until the pressure is on to find someone before a deadline.

Stack the Deck

And then, there's the scenario that plays out like this:

Phone rings. Or—if you're having a particularly bad day—cameras just show up.

REPORTER: "We received a call about Ms. Jones, who says you all aren't helping her. Do you mind talking about this with us?"

The worst thing a group can do is to say "no comment." The silence creates a vacuum in which Ms. Jones is the only voice in the story. Then the story comes out that, indeed, she did not receive the help she needs and the group that's supposed to help isn't talking.

The Ms. Jones scenario should not be seen as something to be feared. It is an opportunity to promote long-term recovery even if it comes wrapped in an untidy package.

Rather than "no comment," ask the reporter to join you. Sit down. Let them record if they are in broadcast media, or take notes if a print journalist. There is no such thing as "off the record" when dealing with the press.

Consider what can be said—and what should be said. Help the reporter to understand that, while you cannot comment on specific cases of need, you can say you are helping _____ number of families in your area with _____ dollars' worth of assistance. You can say that cases are managed and vetted using a certain criteria, and outline what the criteria are. You can also say that you are focused on those who are most vulnerable and that concern for the community sometimes outweighs individual need.

If you find the complaint is valid, it never hurts to tell the reporter you'll check it out. Don't be afraid to get back to a reporter, asking when the deadline may be. And, provide the reporter with a business card or some other way to reach you through immediate contact.

In the end, we cannot control what reporters say or write about our work. What we can control is what is communicated to reporters whenever we interact with them. The message that we put forward as disaster response practitioners should always be positive: one of empowerment, partnership, and responsibility. Arming yourself with facts about your group's capacity, service, and operation is the best way to ensure any negative inquiry has a positive outcome.

＊ ＊ ＊ ＊ ＊

Our family came through Superstorm Sandy incredibly blessed. We survived a week without power, bonded with our new neighbors, and basked in our blessings of safety and security, although so many in our town were not as fortunate. Our son goes to school with families who lost their homes.

Despite our leaky bathtub drain, we prepared for the storm as best we could. The communities we serve in long-term recovery deserve our best effort in preparing for disaster.

QUESTIONS

1. Has your group considered potential areas of unmet needs should a disaster strike? What are some ways to build connections now that may be used should a disaster strike?
2. What are some community social service agencies your long-term recovery group works with? What capacity do those agencies have in the way of connections to local media?
3. Who will handle media inquiries on your team? How will you let everyone in your group know media inquiries should be directed to that person?
4. Should you ever say "no comment" to a reporter? If so, when and why?
5. What's the best way to ensure a negative inquiry has a positive outcome?

7

Nothing Like That Could Ever Happen Here

Lessons Learned from Sandy Hook

ANNE COFFMAN

It seems trite to say that Friday, December 14, 2012 was a beautiful day. The deep blue sky made for a crisp, bright, and altogether perfect mid-December day in Connecticut. My schedule for that day included our annual Christmas lunch for our church staff. Two retired staff members, Ruth and David, planned to meet us at the church to carpool. We hoped an early lunch at a nearby restaurant would beat the holiday rush.

Ruth came in around 11:00 a.m. and mentioned that she had heard on the radio that something was going on in Newtown. Our church in Danbury is less than six miles from Newtown, and we have several members from there, so I went on-line to find out what was happening. The news reports were vague. Then a church member, Lynn, who lives in Newtown, called to tell me that something bad had happened at one of the schools. She thought it was a shooting, but the details were sketchy. We spoke for a few minutes and I promised to pray.

After praying, I was worried, but felt we had little choice but to continue with our lunch plans. The staff of our small church is made up of part-timers who hold other jobs. They had all arranged their schedules to get together that day, and it would be difficult to find another time. Only

---

Anne Coffman is a pastor in Connecticut. She was senior interim minister at the Second Congregational Church in Greenwich when 9/11 deeply affected that community, and she was pastor of Central Christian Church in Danbury when the Sandy Hook Elementary School shootings happened a few miles away.

Ruth and I were aware that anything might be wrong. So we piled into two cars and drove to the restaurant. Everything seemed normal except for my phone, which kept beeping with incoming messages. I had to turn off the sound so that the other diners would not be disturbed.

After finishing lunch and getting everyone back to the church, I finally had a chance to look at my phone and saw a pile of voicemail, texts, and e-mail. Feeling deeply worried, I called Lynn again. She told me that the news was unspeakably bad: twenty children and many teachers at the Sandy Hook Elementary School. All gone. Murdered.

As I heard her words, time seemed to slow down. I thought about my daughter-in-law, a Newtown elementary school teacher on maternity leave; the church member who provided childcare for some Newtown teachers; the long-time friend of my husband who had retired in the Sandy Hook neighborhood. I felt like something deep inside had been ripped open—the same feeling that I had when I heard about the Twin Towers on 9/11. We knew we had been targeted as a people, but we didn't yet understand how this horrific tragedy would affect us as individuals.

* * * * *

When disaster strikes a community, psychological trauma results. The Newtown community had been shattered in a violent way. Twenty first-graders and six educators had been killed. The shooter lay dead in the school. His mother, and seemingly all the answers, were dead in her home nearby.

For most of us, the idea of "school" represents normalcy, safety, and security. Schools are pillars of our communities and our lives as North Americans—we assume and expect that our children will be safe at school. An event like this tears that pillar down.

Tragedies such as Newtown create concentric circles with varying levels of psychological trauma that radiate out from the ground zero of the event. Understanding these circles is at the core of developing appropriate and effective responses for assisting the affected people.

With the Newtown tragedy, the core circle contains those who were at Sandy Hook Elementary School. The people who are actually present at the moment of disaster will always have unique needs, and generalizations about them should be made with great caution.

The second circle includes the families, friends, clergy, and therapeutic caregivers that waited for news at the Sandy Hook Firehouse. This second circle also contains the first responders: the police, the firefighters, and the emergency medical technicians who rushed to the scene to help. While they were always "safe," and therefore not part of the core circle, they have to deal with the raw memories of what they saw and experienced.

The third circle includes the people living in the community where the event occurred. They drive by the school routinely. They are friends and neighbors of the survivors. The fourth circle includes those whose lives intersect with the Newtown community—employers, churches, and childcare providers in surrounding towns. Everyone else is in the fifth circle. They may have intense feelings and reactions relating to the event, but they are distinctly different from people in the other circles.

* * * * *

Three pastoral acts are important following a traumatic event. First, recognize the event and honor its impact by holding mourning rituals such as prayer vigils, community worship services, funerals, and memorial services. Second, return to normal routines as soon as possible. Third, identify or create a safe place for people to be able to emotionally process what has happened.

Emotionally processing does not mean remembering and recounting the details of the tragedy. Everyone reacts to trauma differently. For some people the act of telling their trauma narrative is retraumatizing. To emotionally process a traumatic event means to find a way to fit this unimaginable event into your life, to find ways to feel safe again, and to go on, somehow, with your life. All human beings need to feel safe, and a traumatic event strips away the feeling of safety. It is the lack of an internalized feeling of safety that causes the anxiety, hyper-vigilance, and anger that is often seen in Post-Traumatic Stress Disorder (PTSD).

The normal activities of daily life can be soothing and reassuring. But returning to daily life was a struggle after the Sandy Hook shootings. People in Newtown couldn't run a short errand without experiencing traffic jams caused by the huge influx of people coming to town trying to report, to help, and to understand. They couldn't go to the grocery without being asked by the media about their feelings. In the days following, several school systems in our area called for "lockdowns" because suspicious people had been seen around the school. While such hyper-vigilance is understandable, it had the result of intensifying the psychological trauma for many people.

People who have experienced trauma are easily overwhelmed, and one of the paralyzing circumstances in the days following the Newtown tragedy was the avalanche of gifts that poured into the area. Many people feel they have to respond in a tangible way by giving something. Newtown clergy and community leaders put out word that if anyone felt led to give gifts to the families of the survivors, they should give them instead to needy children and families in their own communities. But despite this, hundreds of teddy bears, quilts, and boxes of candy were sent to Newtown.

They came from all over the world. Many area churches, including my congregation, received boxes of cookies, cards, and toys meant for the survivors of the tragedy. There was no way that all of these gifts could be distributed, and, for many traumatized people, gifts overwhelm more than they provide comfort. Newtown rented a warehouse to hold everything that arrived. Months later most of the gifts still wait.

What *was* helpful were simple expressions of care from people who called and sent e-mails, and the many who assured us of their constant prayer. This was welcome and it was reassuring to know that our community and people were being prayed for. Money also began coming in and the Newtown Savings Bank set up a fund while the United Way of Western Connecticut volunteered to be the contact organization to collect the money. One of our church members was the main organizer of this effort. While debate continues on how to use these financial resources, there is obvious potential for good to be done if we thoughtfully and prayerfully consider the options.

* * * * *

For people who are in a position to provide significant "hands on" support during times of great tragedy, or if something like this ever happens in your community, here are some things that worked well at Newtown.

On the day of the shootings, the medical director and counselors from my church's partner agency, Families and Children's Aid (FCA), went to the firehouse a short distance from Sandy Hook Elementary. This is where the family members waited to learn what had happened. The next day FCA and other agencies established a free, drop-in counseling site at the Reed Middle School in Newtown. A lot of time was spent validating the credentials of the huge number of volunteers who wanted to help. FCA soon developed a three-part method that worked well in providing a safe place for emotional processing. They set up an art room with all kinds of creative materials so people could feel free to create as they needed. They also brought in therapy dogs that had been trained to interact positively with people who are vulnerable or in crisis. Therapy dogs offer unconditional affection that has proven invaluable in people's recovery. There were also counselors available, trained in helping people find ways to recover their sense of safety.

Even with effective methods of treatment, recovery from trauma takes time. Many people in the circles radiating out from Sandy Hook will be recovering for years. Since the shootings, FCA has worked with surviving children and families using play therapy and appropriate children's literature.[1]
Because so many generous individuals and congregations within my own

denomination wanted to reach out to the Newtown community in concrete ways, we worked with our denominational disaster response ministry to provide funds so that FCA could purchase children's books. Thus, this collaboration was between our local congregation, our community partner agency (FCA), and the denominational disaster response fund. We were able to deliver the books that were recommended by FCA and were helpful for children and families trying to make sense of violence and trauma. What was most gratifying was that we, locally, along with FCA, were able to determine for ourselves what would be most useful to our community after the tragedy. This allowed us to direct the denominational disaster funds offered to us in the most helpful ways possible.

* * * * *

The Sandy Hook shooting happened while our church was in the middle of observing Advent. Each of us asked ourselves: Why is the world such a dark place? How can we go on in a world where such terrible things happen? We turned to the scriptures that bring the message of what the coming of Christ means to us, including Isaiah 9:2:

> The people walking in darkness
> have seen a great light;
> on those living in the land of deep darkness
> *a light has dawned.* (NIV)

We remembered the words of Albert Schweitzer:

> At times our own light goes out and is rekindled by a spark from another person. Each of us has cause to think with deep gratitude of those who have lighted the flame within us.

And we repeated to ourselves John's words in the first chapter of his gospel:

> *The light shines in the darkness, and the darkness has not overcome it.*
> (1:5, NIV)

No one in our peaceful, idyllic, New England town would have ever imagined that something like the Sandy Hook tragedy would happen. Not here. But our small church community began to see that, with God's help, the help of the community, and the solidarity and support of our wider church, we can be God's light in the darkness for our traumatized community. By being kind and comforting to each other, continuing to worship, collaborating with partners locally and denominationally, and by praying for our community, we can be a spark that rekindles the flame of hope within another person. We continue to live in the knowledge that each us can be a light shining in the darkness, and the darkness will not be able to overcome it.

Books To Help Young Children Cope with Violence, Disaster, and Loss

A Terrible Thing Happened, by Margaret M. Holmes

Lifetimes: The Beautiful Way to Explain Death to Children, by Bryan Mellonie and Robert Ingpen

One April Morning: Children Remember the Oklahoma City Bombing, by Nancy Lamb and the Children of Oklahoma City

The Fall of Freddie the Leaf, by Leo Buscaglia

The Invisible String, by Patrice Karst

Water Bugs and Dragonflies: Explaining Death to Young Children, by Doris Stickney

QUESTIONS

1. While it is tempting—and perhaps human nature—to believe that a tragedy such as the Sandy Hook shooting will never happen to you or in your community, we know that tragedy occurs when and where we least expect it. How can you prepare yourself and your faith community for such an event?

2. The local congregation in Danbury, Connecticut, was able to work with a community agency in responding to the Sandy Hook tragedy. What are the local organizations and agencies in your community with which you and your congregation could partner? How can you establish a relationship with them (if you haven't already)?

3. After such a tragedy occurs, especially a national tragedy such as Sandy Hook, people are moved to respond in some way. Many of them, as Coffman states, are moved to send material donations (such as toys, teddy bears, quilts, candy, and cookies), rather than sending what is actually needed. What are other creative and more useful ways to respond after such traumatic events?

4. Which passages of scripture would be most comforting to you at such a time? What has been most consoling to you during difficult times in your life?

8

Knowing When to Stay and When to Go

A Guide to Volunteering

JOSH BAIRD

"Go," said a voice in my head. "Go!"

I had been glued to the television and various news or weather-related websites all day, trying to keep up with the latest information about this storm. Initial projections were for a fairly mild hurricane (as hurricanes go); but as the storm slowed down, the dangers rose. Sure enough, levees soon began to overflow, rivers backed up, and neighborhoods that I had come to know and love were inundated. I felt frustrated and helpless, a thousand miles away from the community that, until recently, had been our home, the place where our children were born, and was where so many of the people who are a part of our extended family lived.

"Go," the voice said, getting stronger and more insistent. It took everything I had not to listen to that voice. The urge to jump in the car and head south was nearly overpowering.

It is almost instinctive, the desire to want to help someone in need. When a large disaster strikes a community, we know that help is needed. Most of the time, we have resources to offer. Sometimes, we have skills that are needed. I understand the desire, that instinct, to jump into action, to drive to that community, to do something—anything—to help. Our national media is very good at filling our television screens, front pages,

Josh Baird is an ordained minister in the Christian Church (Disciples of Christ). As director of Disciples Volunteering, he facilitates opportunities to participate in long-term disaster recovery efforts and other service for volunteers from across North America.

46

and Internet sites with compelling images and stories of people in need. How can we, as a people of faith, not respond?

But, most of the time, the worst thing we can do is listen to that voice that tells us to immediately "Go!"

Among disaster responders, people who just show up to help are called "unaffiliated volunteers" or "spontaneous volunteers." Other words, however, get more quickly to the point, among them "distraction," "headache," and "nuisance." The fact is that just about anybody who shows up to help arrives needing something. Not everyone thinks about whether there will be places to buy gas, food, and water in a disaster zone. Many people arrive without tools, rather assuming they will be made available. Almost everyone arrives needing a place to stay and something to do.

I have had the privilege of sitting down with pastors and local leaders after disaster has hit their community. They tell amazing stories about how the community rallied in response. "We pulled together and took care of each other," is a common refrain. These stories also typically include a few details about people who came from out of the area to help. Sometimes, these spontaneous volunteers called first to ask if their help was needed. Sometimes, they called as more of a "courtesy" to inform folks that help was on the way. Even if they had the real courtesy to ask, however, most pastors and community leaders do not say, "No." But they should.

The task of finding something for spontaneous volunteers to do often falls on our pastors. Most take this on because they think they should, even though they have much more important work to do, such as checking on church members and being available to the wider local community, not to mention taking care of themselves and their own families. After one disaster, I met with several church leaders and told them it was okay to say "No" to all the offers of help that they were receiving. The mood in the room shifted, as if a weight had been lifted. One pastor then admitted that she would much rather be helping the people of her church connect with relatives or find a place to stay than arrange work or housing for yet another out-of-town mission team. It is common for more people to spontaneously show up than can possibly be accommodated. In these circumstances, people spend a lot of time standing around or searching for something to do; sometimes, they're even turned away. The question we should all be asking, in circumstances such as these, is: Whose needs am I really trying to meet?

The same question is also appropriate before we begin gathering donations to send to the disaster zone. Unfortunately, some people use a disaster as an excuse to clean out their garages or the back of their closets. Threadbare clothes; used underwear; random, expired, even unlabeled prescription medicines; old, half-empty cans of paint; broken Christmas lights and other junk: all of this stuff and more pours into communities following a disaster. The time it takes to sift through it all to determine whether there is anything worth keeping is time that is not spent working with people who need help. The space that must be found to sort, store, and display or dispose of these things becomes a burden when space is already at a premium. After the city of Joplin, Missouri, was struck by a tornado, I remember a story in the news about how communities in Alabama, which had been hit by multiple tornados less than four weeks earlier, were sending donations on to Joplin. In my head, I imagined a convoy of semis hauling donated junk that nobody wanted from one disaster to another.

News media are good at laying bare the devastation of a disaster. The stories and images they share move us to want to help. Only in recent years have they begun to tell the other side of that story: that not all help is helpful, and that sometimes it only increases the burden on a community that is still reeling. Communities that are hit hard by disaster depend on outside assistance for their recovery. But with the exception of professional services offered by trained First Responders and organizations such as the Red Cross, the kind of assistance that is needed while the television cameras are still there is limited.

In the immediate hours and days following a disaster, trained responders are saving lives and meeting the most basic of needs: providing shelter, food, water, and medical care to those who have been directly affected. These services occur during the emergency phase of disaster response.[1] The phases of a disaster and an appropriate response are not clearly separated. The emergency response often begins while the disaster is still occurring. And it typically continues after relief begins. Once basic survival needs are met, attention turns to securing property. Damaged roofs get the blue tarp treatment; downed trees are cut and hauled to the curb; flooded homes have water-logged carpet—and sometimes furnishings, clothes, flooring, and walls—removed so the homes can dry. During this relief phase, neighbors are most needed as people pitch in together and folks who can come and go—and who know the local area—are most useful.

This need for neighbors provides an exception to the "don't go" rule. If people can get to a community hit by disaster in half a day or less—taking into account road hazards, closures, detours, and other unpredictable conditions—then their presence *may* be helpful. They can get there, work for about half a day, and still get home that night. They also must be completely self-sufficient, carrying all of the tools, protective gear, sunscreen, bug spray, food, gas, and cash necessary, plus two to three

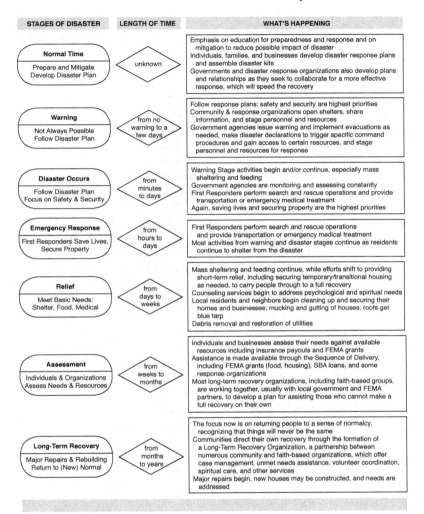

STAGES OF DISASTER	LENGTH OF TIME	WHAT'S HAPPENING
Normal Time Prepare and Mitigate Develop Disaster Plan	unknown	Emphasis on education for preparedness and response and on mitigation to reduce possible impact of disaster Individuals, families, and businesses develop disaster response plans and assemble disaster kits Governments and disaster response organizations also develop plans and relationships as they seek to collaborate for a more effective response, which will speed the recovery
Warning Not Always Possible Follow Disaster Plan	from no warning to a few days	Follow response plans; safety and security are highest priorities Community & response organizations open shelters, share information, and stage personnel and resources Government agencies issue warning and implement evacuations as needed, make disaster declarations to trigger specific command procedures and gain access to certain resources, and stage personnel and resources for response
Disaster Occurs Follow Disaster Plan Focus on Safety & Security	from minutes to days	Warning Stage activities begin and/or continue, especially mass sheltering and feeding Government agencies are monitoring and assessing constantly First Responders perform search and rescue operations and provide transportation or emergency medical treatment Again, saving lives and securing property are the highest priorities
Emergency Response First Responders Save Lives, Secure Property	from hours to days	First Responders perform search and rescue operations and provide transportation or emergency medical treatment Most activities from warning and disaster stages continue as residents continue to shelter from the disaster
Relief Meet Basic Needs: Shelter, Food, Medical	from days to weeks	Mass sheltering and feeding continue, while efforts shift to providing short-term relief, including securing temporary/transitional housing as needed, to carry people through to a full recovery Counseling services begin to address psychological and spiritual needs Local residents and neighbors begin cleaning up and securing their homes and businesses; mucking and gutting of houses; roofs get blue tarp Debris removal and restoration of utilities
Assessment Individuals & Organizations Assess Needs & Resources	from weeks to months	Individuals and businesses assess their needs against available resources including insurance payouts and FEMA grants Assistance is made available through the Sequence of Delivery, including FEMA grants (food, housing), SBA loans, and some response organizations Most long-term recovery organizations, including faith-based groups, are working together, usually with local government and FEMA partners, to develop a plan for assisting those who cannot make a full recovery on their own
Long-Term Recovery Major Repairs & Rebuilding Return to (New) Normal	from months to years	The focus now is on returning people to a sense of normalcy, recognizing that things will never be the same Communities direct their own recovery through the formation of a Long-Term Recovery Organization, a partnership between numerous community and faith-based organizations, which offer case management, unmet needs assistance, volunteer coordination, spiritual care, and other services Major repairs begin, new houses may be constructed, and needs are addressed

times the amount of water or sports drink needed. Anyone meeting all of these conditions still must check to see whether people are even being allowed into the community, or if a curfew is in effect, before loading their vehicles. Finally, they must have a point of contact—a place to go or a person they've already connected with—before setting out.

For the rest of us, those who are more than a few hours' drive away, the waiting can be difficult. In the next phase of the recovery, things seem to slow down. Most of the people impacted by the disaster, and the government, civic, and faith-based organizations involved in the response are, in reality, extremely busy assessing needs, gathering resources, and planning for the long term.[2] Homeowners begin to file with their insurance companies. FEMA focuses on registering people who may need assistance and guiding them through various assistance programs as appropriate. Local governments, community organizations, churches, and other agencies begin working to develop the infrastructure needed to support a long-term response.

Both the individual and organizational work can take several months to complete. Communities, therefore, are not typically ready for out-of-town mission teams in any significant number until at least three months after the disaster. When they are, the response shifts into the recovery phase. This gives those who want to "Go!" and help plenty of time to plan appropriately and make a trip when their service is most needed. Rest assured, unmet needs in the community will long outlast the headlines and news crews. The longer the recovery takes, the more important mission teams will become. The most important thing we can do with that desire to "Go!" is channel it into planning a trip many months, even a year, into the future. Tap into the desire and the energy of your friends and neighbors at home, work, school, and church and make a commitment while the story is still hot to go when interest will have cooled.

At the same time, appropriate donations are needed, and giving is one important response to disaster. To organize or participate in a drive for needed donations, follow a few basic guidelines. Make sure your donations have a destination before you give them. Find out what is really needed. If you wouldn't want it yourself, don't send it to someone else. And never, ever send clothes (unless they are specifically requested—and then, send only new clothing).

Another option is to assemble cleanup buckets or other kits for Church World Service.[3] These kits are collected year round and stored in a warehouse. When disaster strikes, they are quickly shipped into communities so that folks have the basic cleaning supplies they need to clean up their homes. Large disasters quickly deplete the supply of cleanup buckets available. So, while the buckets assembled after one disaster may not make it to the affected community this time, they are vital for replenishing stock and ensuring that there are enough buckets ready to go to the next time they are needed.

If you still feel the urge to clean something out, skip the garage and the closet—and go straight to your purse or wallet. The best donation after any disaster is a financial donation. Cash allows responders to flexibly adapt to meet the obvious and the unanticipated needs that arise after a disaster. When an unexpected semi arrives hauling pallets of water, funds can be shifted to purchase food or materials. When a family walks through the door of a relief center needing gas for their generator, a gift card can be given. When a group of people are ready to climb roofs and install tarps but a decent ladder can't be located, one can be purchased. Through ecumenical contacts as well as historic and emerging partners, mainline denominations participate in strong response networks. Through these relationships, financial gifts made to each denomination's disaster response offering and Church World Service[4] are immediately available for critical needs. Other grants are targeted to support the work of response partners as they prepare for the long-term recovery.

There are a few more things we can do after a disaster. We can be in prayer—for those who have been affected by the disaster, for those who are responding, and for many, many more to respond when the time is right. We can care enough to follow the response beyond the headlines, to continue to seek information about what's really happening, and look for creative, appropriate ways to respond. And we can take advantage of the attention being paid to this disaster to prepare our families, church, and community should a disaster hit close to home. If we do these things, share as we are able, and don't go there until our presence is needed, we will truly be responding at our best.

Once the national media gets its first, happy story about how people are beginning their recovery, they will go home. This is when the work is just getting started. This is when you are most needed. This is when the Church has the greatest opportunity to be the hands, the feet, and the heart of Jesus, offering help, hope, and healing with our neighbors. May we faithfully aim to arrive when we are needed, to serve as we are able, and to be among the last to leave.

RESOURCES

1. CWS Clean-up Bucket list – http://www.churchworldservice.org/site/PageServer?pagename=kits_emergency
2. CWS starting page for all Kits and Bucket list –http://www.churchworldservice.org/site/PageServer?pagename=kits_main
3. Flow Chart for Sequence of Delivery – http://www.fema.gov/pdf/about/regions/regioni/sequence2008.pdf

QUESTIONS

1. Name three phases of disaster recovery. What kind of help is most needed during each phase?

2. When is a community ready to receive large numbers of out-of-town mission teams?
3. When is the best time to begin planning a mission trip to aid in the recovery?
4. How can your congregation assist with a recovery that is close to home? What can you do when the disaster is farther away?

ONCE THE CAMERAS LEAVE
Long-Term Recovery

The Long-Term Recovery Process and Your Faith Community

Some Starting Points

JOSH BAIRD AND SANDRA KENNEDY-OWES

The storm has passed. The floodwaters have receded. The fire has been extinguished. Neighbors have been out in force doing what neighbors do best—helping one another. The response efforts of local governments, faith communities, civic groups, and social service agencies are in motion addressing the immediate needs of families and individuals affected by the disaster. Television crews, newspaper reporters, and other members of the media have been out taking pictures and telling stories of the survivors for the last few days, but now they are beginning to pack up. The adrenaline rush is subsiding, the stories are fewer and, frankly, less exciting as most people shift their focus to securing and cleaning their homes, with some thought toward repairs and recovery.

The people impacted, wanting nothing more than to return to normal, begin to draw upon whatever resources they have or have access to. These resources might include insurance, personal finances, family assistance, building materials, physical labor, and, in the case of a federally-declared disaster, additional funding. In the months that follow, many will find that they are nowhere near to being "back to normal." With their resources exhausted, many folks will still need assistance completing their recovery.

Sandra Kennedy-Owes serves as an emergency response specialist for Church World Service, helping to train communities in long-term recovery basics.

Josh Baird is director of Disciples Volunteering, a ministry of the Christian Church (Disciples of Christ) that helps connect volunteers to long-term recovery opportunities.

While there was much to do early on to assist with immediate relief, it is at this moment that a shared community response is needed most.

What Happens Next?

The process of disaster recovery begins before a disaster even threatens to strike. This recovery process has taken shape through decades of collaborative response efforts as a means to help people rebuild their homes and their lives after disaster, and it continues to evolve for each phase of a disaster.

Preparedness is a critical phase of the process for any community and should be pursued during normal (non-disaster) times. If there is advance notice of a potential or imminent disaster, people have the benefit of a warning phase to initiate individual and community safety plans. If there is no warning, preparedness plans are put into action the moment disaster strikes, in what is called the impact phase. As soon as first responders are able, they begin their work of saving lives. This constitutes the emergency phase, throughout which preparedness plans are followed as people focus on maintaining safety, shelter, and security. As the emergency response wanes, the relief phase begins. This is marked by meeting basic needs for food, shelter, and medical care as well as securing property, usually by applying temporary corrections to disaster-related damage (for example, securing a blue tarp on a damaged roof to stop further water intrusion). It is a time of frenzied activity, and its passage truly can be marked by the steady disappearance of news crews from the community.

When immediate needs have been met in a way that provides a short-term solution, the recovery shifts to an assessment phase: people determine the extent of their needs and take stock of available resources. At the same time, organizations who want to participate in the recovery determine what resources they can contribute, assess their capacity to help, and solidify plans for partnering to address unmet needs. Long-term recovery, then, is the phase of disaster response during which a community implements these plans and structures, helping affected individuals, families, and communities work toward a "new normal." Long-term recovery goes beyond relief and initial cleanup to the actual rebuilding of homes and lives. Depending on the size and scope of the disaster, the long-term recovery phase is likely to last months or even years. This is a time and an opportunity for communities to grow back better, stronger, and healthier through cooperation, communication, coordination, and collaboration.[1]

If organizations within the community have collectively planned and prepared for a recovery, the assessment phase can proceed fairly quickly: relationships are already in place that can be built upon; plans of action and memoranda of understanding that have already been agreed upon can be implemented. Unfortunately, too many communities have not proactively completed a plan for a coordinated, whole-community response, which results in the planning and implementation of a long-term recovery process taking more time. It often leads to a pivotal moment when organizations, including faith communities, consider whether to respond on their own rather than engage in what feels like a painstakingly slow process of partnering with others.

Motivated by a strong desire to capitalize on the momentum achieved during the relief phase and uncertain exactly how to proceed in partnership, some organizations may choose to make their own plans. By operating on their own, they are choosing, essentially, to meet whatever needs they are able to with whatever resources their own organization has available or has the capacity to raise. This constant meeting of needs fosters a feeling of success and can have the unfortunate effect of drawing attention and resources away from the cooperative response that should now be in formation. Regardless, it only prolongs the inevitable: organizations that go it alone often find that their resources dwindle more quickly, their leaders burn out sooner, and their ability to assist the community recovery ends long before the recovery does. These organizations, operating on their own, may not reflect the priorities of the community. They will also be limited in their ability to verify the needs and resources of those who seek help, thereby running the risk of either duplicating services or not channeling their support to those with the greatest need. For these reasons and others, it is not advisable for any organization, including a congregation, to attempt to conduct a long-term recovery on its own.

The alternative is a recovery process in which a community comes together to identify and use the resources of survivors, community stakeholders, multiple levels of government, and many other partners for advancing a shared recovery. This ensures that members of the community establish priorities for addressing the needs of affected individuals and families, especially the most vulnerable, so that through their recovery they may sustain their physical, social, economic, and spiritual well-being.[2] Traditionally, churches, synagogues, mosques, temples, other houses of worship, and religiously affiliated service organizations have been the cornerstone of any shared recovery, primarily because these groups are usually present before a disaster and have a track record for providing other services, aid, and resources. They are uniquely positioned to serve an important role in moving the community toward a new normal.

The question now is: How can a wide array of organizations partner together to help their community after a disaster? Local communities that have experienced disaster and found themselves needing long-term help have learned, with the assistance of regional and national organizations, that the best way to pull together to meet the remaining needs of people affected by the disaster is through the formation of a Long-term Recovery Group.

What Is a Long-term Recovery Group?

A Long-term Recovery Group (LTRG) is a cooperative body consisting of representatives from faith-based, non-profit, government, business, civic, social service, and other organizations working within a community to assist individuals and families as they recover from a disaster.[3] The specific structure adopted by a LTRG and the ways in which it will live out its mission will vary, based on the needs of the affected community and the partners who are supporting the recovery. In fact, determining the form and function of the overall LTRG and its subgroupings (or subcommittees) is a crucial way that the local community owns and directs its recovery. Whether they choose to organize as a Long-term Recovery Organization (LTRO), Long-term Recovery Committee (LTRC), an Unmet Needs Committee, an Interfaith Committee, a Roundtable, or something else, will be determined by local leaders based on local needs and resources.

A well-organized LTRG can

- Ensure available resources are used for the recovery
- Engage a wide variety of local and national partners
- Set goals and standards appropriate for its community
- Monitor progress as needs are met and work to overcome gaps and roadblocks when they are not met
- Identify inequalities and deficiencies in the recovery and advocate for a just response
- Provide for the spiritual and emotional care of survivors, caregivers, and the community
- Help the community adjust to a new normal

The best way to organize to meet these needs is to divide into working groups or subcommittees. Partners will focus on having representation with the subcommittee(s) that best fits with the resources they have to offer. Community members with relevant skills may also be active at the subcommittee level, offering their time and experience to help move the recovery forward. A LTRG breaks a community's long-term recovery into a variety of components, typically forming subcommittees to focus on some or all of the following:

Case management is critical to any recovery. The LTRG sets the priorities and guidelines for providing assistance to those affected by the disaster. Trained case managers (paid and/or volunteer) then assess and prioritize the needs of people seeking assistance and connect them with available resources based on the guidelines of the LTRG.

A subgroup committed to resource development works to access resources from within the community and beyond. This may include financial gifts or grants from nonprofit, corporate, and individual donors. In-kind donations are also commonly sought, including everything from building materials to new appliances. A donations management committee develops a plan for storing or disbursing these resources between the various partner agencies of the LTRG. If it is warranted, the LTRG may even secure warehouse space, to be managed by this committee.

A major piece of any recovery is helping people with significant repairs to their homes; sometimes it is even necessary to rebuild homes completely. It is helpful to have a construction management team in place to ensure that such work, especially when performed by volunteers, is up to local codes and standards.

Volunteer coordination is essential to ensure that those who offer their time and labor for the recovery are enabled to serve in the best possible way. Included among the tasks this group can pursue are: determining the capacity of the LTRG and its members to provide work for volunteers and controlling the number of daily/weekly volunteers accordingly; lining up and coordinating housing for out-of-town work teams; and matching the skills of those offering assistance with the work that needs to be done .

Another role of the LTRG is to enhance community recognition of the recovery. A communications team can tell the story of the recovery and raise awareness in the community, the region, and beyond. By using existing relationships or building new ones with representatives of local media outlets, this group creates a platform for lifting up ongoing needs, for celebrating achievements, for commemorating anniversaries; in short, for reminding those inside and outside of a community that the recovery continues. When debris is no longer visible and the spotlight begins to move on, the LTRG must continue to communicate that the recovery is far from over.

A variety of spiritual and emotional care needs exist after a disaster. To make matters more complicated, these needs change over time. In long-term recovery, every effort is made to address the needs of individuals and families from a holistic approach looking at various needs beyond the physical rebuilding of a home. It is common for faith communities to participate through this committee. The needs that are addressed include those not only of survivors but also of caregivers, who often must be reminded to take care of themselves while they are taking care of others. This committee also helps with the communications committee to shape appropriate commemorations such as anniversaries or significant recovery milestones by operating with a special awareness for the potential triggers and trauma that such events can spark. Ultimately, spiritual care providers from a variety of traditions and mental health providers from an affected community can foster a sense of hope among those affected.[4]

After any disaster, there is always the possibility of some needs being overlooked in the immediate and long-term response plan. It is also possible that local regulations or practices that are important in normal conditions may impede or undermine recovery in post-disaster circumstances. For a given community, a group focused on advocacy can ensure that a particular neighborhood, community, or vulnerable population is fairly treated in a widespread disaster. Advocacy can also take place within a community's political and administrative structure to assure that sufficient resources are devoted to recovery, mitigation, and resiliency projects. This is another committee where the church and other faith communities can serve on behalf of those affected, raising a voice to help assure that the unmet needs of all people are considered, even on a case-by-case basis as necessary.

Please note, these descriptions are not meant to be prescriptive or exhaustive, but are offered as an overview of some of the roles that the various working groups of a LTRG might pursue. The actual structure and role of a LTRG and its subgroups should be determined by the community, based on its resources (including participating organizations) and its needs. While LTRGs primarily consist of community volunteers and representatives of nonprofits, having good relationships with local, state, and federal government agencies is vital to their success. Government agents are often able to help navigate various requirements for repairs and rebuilding and access certain financial resources. Businesses and civic groups are also important contributors as they look for ways to help the community recover. They often have financial and in-kind resources to share. Businesses and civic groups may also have access to volunteer pools. Large businesses in the community can work with their regional and national headquarters to channel outside resources to the community.

Faith communities also have unique resources to offer to a recovery. As your faith community explores participating in a long-term recovery, consider the resources that it can bring to the table. These resources may include volunteers, money, equipment, training, and other skills that could contribute to the rebuilding and recovery process. Begin by asking several questions of your group:

1. Are any members trained, by the church or by recognized disaster organizations, in disaster response?
2. Does the church raise money to respond to disasters? Are those funds available to be committed to the long-term recovery?
3. Has the church developed any response/recovery teams?
4. Has the church acquired tools or related resources, such as generators, tool trailers, and shower trailers?
5. Could the church facilities, or some portion of them, be appropriate for housing out of town work teams?

All of the above resources are essential during recovery and can be offered as part of the church's response. The most important resource in most congregations is its people. What skills do church members possess? Are there carpenters, brick masons, roofers, plumbers, electricians, painters, or other skilled laborers who are willing to volunteer their time to the church and recovery group? What about administrators, social workers, chaplains, or counselors? Does your church have retirees who can make phone calls and send e-mails? Are there individuals with important ties to community organizations or officials? Church members can plug into any appropriate subcommittee of the LTRG and use their relationships to recruit others within the wider community to actively engage as well.

Churches with a denominational affiliation can also attract and leverage denominational resources to increase support for the LTRG. This may provide access to a larger denominational volunteer pool as well as response grants for the LTRG. Your denomination may also have resources to help your faith community shape and strengthen its participation in the recovery. In addition, a good variety of resources are available from other faith groups, ecumenical bodies, and disaster response organizations; a list of related resources is found in the "Toolkit" section of this book.

Helping rebuild one's own community can be incredibly rewarding, and faith communities have long been key contributors to long term recovery. By pooling resources and building relationships, churches and other groups can put their faith into action in efficient, effective ways and help an entire community heal.

Some of the information in this essay was originally published in Church World Service's Long-term Recovery Basics/Getting Organized *and its* Community Arise Disaster Ministry Curriculum *as well as National Voluntary Organizations Active in Disaster's* Long-term Recovery Guide. *These three volumes are excellent resources containing more detail for launching a Long Term Recovery Group.*

10

Creating Holy Space for Volunteer Efforts

SUSAN LASALLE

"What is a mission station?"

That is exactly the question that the members of First Christian Church (Disciples of Christ) of Slidell, Louisiana, and I asked in the months following Hurricane Katrina. We had never heard of such a thing. We certainly had never been part of such a thing. So, what is it? How do we do open one? What needs to be done before, during, and after opening a Mission Station? When our denominational disaster response fund and volunteer ministries asked First Christian Church of Slidell to host volunteer mission groups coming to our area to help with hurricane recovery efforts, our congregation agreed to play a part in the vast and vital work of ministering to the people and communities impacted by the hurricane even though we weren't sure what we were agreeing to exactly. Soon enough, our denominational staff explained that we were needed to provide a place where volunteers could shower, sleep, and eat. The details were up to us.

So my congregation and I waded into this unknown territory. We found ourselves asking, "What is it that we would want or need if we were away from home helping a town recover or rebuild?" We knew that we did

Susan Lasalle is a regional field staff member for Church World Service. From 2005 to 2013 she served as pastor of First Christian Church in Slidell, Louisiana. First Christian Church has served as a mission station, housing over 1,200 volunteers over the last eight years following Hurricane Katrina.

not have a lot of space for a Mission Station, but we also knew we would do the best we could to serve God and our community.

The first steps were technical. After the hurricane, we were without electrical power in the fellowship hall for about six months, so we had to wait until power was restored. Then we got to work. We installed a shower; made sure our appliances were in good, working order; and checked the air conditioning and heating systems to make sure they were functioning properly.

The next steps concerned atmosphere and aesthetics. We considered what mission groups would really enjoy when they came to stay with us, and created an environment that was conducive to recharging for the next day's work. We provided basic television, board games, and various types of reading material. We developed separate spaces for sleeping, dining, and fellowship by hanging tarpaulins as dividers. In the process of getting ready to welcome volunteers, we also formed a team to greet each group when they arrived, join with them in prayer, and host a brief orientation. We provided maps of the area, picture and informational books about Hurricane Katrina, and, since Slidell is only twenty minutes from New Orleans, a set of brochures highlighting area attractions. One of our members brought the local newspaper so groups could get a sense of the area, its people, and its culture.

We soon discovered that one important opportunity of a Mission Station was to share with the volunteers our own personal experiences of Hurricane Katrina. We also knew that people coming to the New Orleans area would want to enjoy delicious Cajun and Creole cuisine and delectable seafood, so we decided that on the Tuesdays we were hosting a mission group, our church would provide a home-cooked, Louisiana-style meal, complete with a time for fellowship and conversation. Perhaps more than any other aspect of the Mission Station, the volunteers enjoyed these Tuesday nights. We exchanged stories about our lives, our churches, our communities, and our God. When groups left, they always made comments as to how precious the Tuesday night meal was, because of the good food and the blessed fellowship.

We now have three journals filled with comments that tell us just how sacred the volunteers considered their entire time at the station. Each group was invited to share memories, stories, a word about their ministry in the area. We have joyfully housed over 1200 volunteers from 27 states, 82 churches, and seven denominations.

Over the seven years that we have served as a Mission Station, our congregation can now answer that question we asked back in the spring of 2006: "What is a Mission Station?"

A Mission Station is a place where the body of Christ comes together to serve a community devastated by disaster. It's a place where people with a heart to serve can reside for a time to carry out the work of mission. It's a place where volunteers can find rest and nourishment for their bodies and souls; where God's hospitality is lived out and discovered in tangible, meaningful ways; and where volunteers can find personal and communal time with God.

These are the aspects of a Mission Station that our congregation, First Christian Church of Slidell, has learned and practiced. The facilities and methods of Mission Stations will vary from location to location. But the basic elements of hospitality, grace, love, and ministry together will characterize the Mission Station regardless of where it is located, or the disaster and recovery to which its volunteers are responding.

From our congregation's perspective, operating a Mission Station has inspired us to become more involved in our community and to build stronger ecumenical relationships. It has breathed new life into our church and helped us grow spiritually. Finally, a Mission Station is a gift from God and to God, for God's people and to God's people—an expression of hospitality in the midst of suffering and loss. Hosting a Mission Station is a calling and an act of worship. It is a source of joy—a true blessing— for its hosts, volunteers, and the community it serves.

QUESTIONS

1. Does your church facility have appropriate features to host volunteers if a disaster strikes your community? If not, what might your congregation need to add, build, or give up?
2. Based on this essay and Josh Baird's essay on volunteering, how long after a disaster strikes do you think a church should wait until opening a Mission Station in an affected area? What partnerships should a church develop before hosting volunteers?
3. Have you ever stayed at a Disaster Mission Station? What made it a hospitable space? What would you have changed about your experience?
4. For how long a period of time do you think a Mission Station should commit to hosting volunteers?

11

How Vulnerable Populations Are Affected by Disasters

RUAMA CAMP

Disasters are not equal-opportunity events. The truth is that disasters affect different segments of the population in different ways.

Who Are Vulnerable Populations?

Since the 2005 Gulf Coast hurricanes, emergency response experts have placed a new focus on disaster preparedness and response to better protect vulnerable populations. Vulnerable populations are groups that have noted deficiencies. The most vulnerable among us are often those people who need special protection: namely, women, children, the elderly, people with disabilities, minority populations, the homeless, and those living in poverty or low-income situations.

When disaster strikes, the social and economic needs of these groups are magnified. Disenfranchised communities struggle with getting across the hurdles of recovery. Those hurdles include, but are not limited to:

- Pre-disaster damage
- Inadequate insurance (or no insurance at all)
- Lack of resource knowledge
- Distrust of governmental agencies

Ruama Camp started her disaster journey in 2001 in Houston, Texas, as a local hire for FEMA in the Voluntary Agency Department. Afterwards, she led Tropical Storm Allison relief efforts in Houston and was later employed by FEMA as a disaster assistance employee (DAE) in the Voluntary Agency Department as a FEMA VAL. She is founder and director for GRACE Community Services, the first African American–founded disaster case management and education ministry in the country.

- Church leaders not familiar with how to participate before, during, and after a disaster strikes
- Being members of nonmainline denominations in congregations that are often quite small, with no aid available
- Lack of additional cash on hand
- No emergency fund
- Lack of understanding regarding the FEMA Sequence of Delivery
- Skepticism regarding strangers' motivation to help
- Pride

According to the United Nations' Hyogo Framework for Action,[1] disasters affect over 200 million people annually, causing significant loss of life, forced migration, and disruption of livelihoods and institutions. The trend over the past 15–20 years points to a greater frequency of environmental, climatic, political, and economic hazards—and, therefore, a growing risk for vulnerable populations worldwide. Though disasters affect everyone, often the impact disproportionately falls on poor countries and the poor and marginalized people within. Thus, the effects of disasters are not simply a humanitarian problem, but also a major challenge for emergency response long-term workers (case management, long-term recovery groups, and volunteer teams).

Outreach and Challenges

Different strategies and tools are available to community leaders and laypersons, such as community planning sessions, disaster training, mock exercises, and training specifically for youth. Community Emergency Response Teams (CERT), local agencies such as G.R.A.C.E. Community Services, and others have developed grassroots efforts of disaster training for local communities. To ensure vulnerable populations' participation in the recovery process, the message has to resonate, speak to, or, ideally, come from them to get others' attention within their community. As I have engaged in disaster preparedness, I have often noticed that outreach materials distributed to vulnerable populations often do not use images that resonate with those communities. Moreover, underfunded social service agencies and an overall lack in infrastructure mean that disseminating the information in these communities is often difficult, therefore causing them to be in disarray at the onset of disaster.

When disaster strikes in those communities of need, those working to respond must be willing to embrace the "*NOW*" of the situation: be mindful that your assumptions may not be correct, and be willing to adapt. When people are seen as solely responsible for their life circumstances due only to bad choices that they have made (as is generally the case when relating to substance abusers, unwed mothers, minorities, ex-offenders, and those living in poverty), there is less public compassion and frequently a stigma surrounding those groups. When disaster strikes in the areas where vulnerable populations live, it is important not to bring one's own biases into the recovery zone. The recovery zone should be a safe haven for those who have gone through a natural or human-caused disaster. One's assumptions about a population—Are they victims of circumstance or just lazy? Are they givers or takers in our society?—should have no role in how resources are distributed.

When most disasters happen, at least 10 to 15 percent of an affected population will not be able to recover on its own. With this in mind, as a disaster caretaker, it is imperative that you show up on the scene ready to assess the damage and its effects on the community, and that you stand ready to assist in returning survivors to their predisaster condition. Many times the victims may receive assistance that leaves them better off than they were predisaster; it's easy to fall into the trap of feeling judgmental when this happens. However, I always suggest that volunteers have a different attitude. "It could've been me!" is always a good reminder to us.

Understanding how recovery works is critical in disaster recovery. Getting the right information helps give clarity and confidence that enables effective advocacy for resources for the survivors. Good stewardship requires knowing the facts and not prejudging; it also requires familiarity with the FEMA Sequence of Delivery (the protocol for appropriately accessing FEMA resources, including grants and low-interest loans) and the guidelines of faith-based and other agencies providing services. Find out what the survivors' lives were like before the storm, and help them access services for which they are eligible. All caregivers must remember that part of their work is helping those affected maintain their sense of dignity. Proverbs 18:21 says, "Death and life are in the power of the tongue" (CEB). How we communicate with people can make all the difference in their recovery process.

Keep in mind, too, that an assumption and an assessment are not the same thing. A family arriving at an evacuation shelter dressed in designer clothing may have lost everything except the clothes on their back. Ask questions and leave judgment at the door. Everyone who enters the recovery zone must be treated compassionately. Make sure you have identified the true need; not what you want or think, but what the individual needs. Sometimes those needs will be informed by the community context. Don't give flowers to someone who needs shoes. If volunteers learn how to respond to needs as presented, and push beyond their own preconceived notions about vulnerable populations, they will not only help change lives, but will themselves have a life-changing experience. They will experience a feeling of accomplishment and not defeat. That's when you know you have served with the hands of God.

QUESTIONS

1. What is a "Vulnerable Population"? What characteristics make some communities more vulnerable than others?
2. How might a disaster affect communities differently? What factors impact a community's ability to recover?
3. Camp states, "One's assumptions about a population—Are they victims of circumstance or just lazy? Are they givers or takers in our society?—should have no role in how resources are distributed." What do you understand to be the proper criteria for distributing resources following a disaster?
4. Are you familiar with FEMA's Sequence of Delivery? What do economically vulnerable communities need to know about it?

12

Environmental Issues and Disaster Recovery

The church has an impressive record of responding to human needs following natural disasters—stepping in with incredible knowledge, resources, and hard work to rebuild communities that have been devastated, whether by hurricane, earthquake, flood, fire, or tornado. Around the world, the church often gives critical leadership to the first response on the ground, as well as providing volunteers and professionals who stay the longest, making sure the community gets back on its feet.

However, the impacts of natural disasters are not limited to humanity. Eco-systems that support all kinds of life are damaged. Furthermore, the human impact on the environment often compounds the impact of a disaster. Bodies of water become polluted through run-off. Once-contained chemicals seep into the water supply. Mudslides and flooding become more common as natural barriers are stripped away.

The impact of Hurricane Katrina was felt not just by people but by the wetlands that run along the Gulf Coast, and the aquatic life in them. The impact was also exacerbated by the damage that had been done to the wetlands through pollution and run-off over generations. The earthquake in Haiti is another example. Vast logging and deforestation across the country removed the root systems that would typically hold

---

Jordan Bles served the National Council of Churches, USA, Eco-Justice Program from 2007 to 2010 as assistant director and coordinator of western land protection. Part of his work included encouraging people of faith to consider how climate change affects their core ministries, such as disaster response, and how that reality should impact the ways ministry is carried out.

the soil together, significantly exacerbating damage to the island and its ecosystems following the earthquake.

Natural disasters can lead us to consider how the way we live furthers the devastation wrought by disaster. They also give us a chance to rebuild in ways that demonstrate a more balanced relationship with the environment and create sustainable communities that respect God's creation.

Following a disaster, we can rebuild our communities in a "green" way, starting with the materials used in construction. Are we selecting supplies that enable our buildings to conserve energy and not have as great an impact on the environment? Are we using materials that are largely recycled?

We can also look at the ways our communities are designed. Are we designing in ways that are less car-centered? Are our communities laid out to take advantage of natural sources of water and energy? Are we creating intentional spaces in our communities to remind us of our connection with the rest of the environment, preserving green spaces and other natural beauty? Are new food systems sustainable, or do farms continue to utilize large amounts of pesticides, leading to toxic run-off and environmental damage?

One example of what this can look like is the city of Greensburg, Kansas. Greensburg was devastated by a tornado in 2007. When planning how to rebuild, the city was determined to consider environmental impact and issues. The buildings were constructed to meet government Leadership in Energy & Environmental Design (LEED)[1] standards in terms of energy efficiency, and the town is now powered by wind turbines.[2] Greensburg's leaders demonstrated how to rebuild in a way that lessens the impact on the environment, and perhaps even decreases the frequency and severity of natural disasters themselves. Natural disasters can also lead us to consider our relationship with the rest of the environment around us, and seek to rebuild it, too. We can replant forests where they once existed. We can restore wetlands so that our communities are better protected. We can restore habitats for species that are native to the area. It is an opportunity to enter into a deeper worship of the One who created our world; to consider how we fit and how to live in right, sustainable relationship with all of it. Creation Justice Ministries (creationjustice. org) has resources has resources that can help us consider our impact on waterways and wildlife, and plan how we might rebuild and restore some of these places. Liturgical and theological resources are available to help incorporate this into worship.[3]

It might seem inappropriate to say that a disaster is a horrible thing to waste, but when it comes to working for the restoration of the environment, it is true. Disasters give the church a chance to be the church. We have an amazing track record in how we respond to the human cost and toll—feeding, housing, and rebuilding. We also have a chance to lead and witness to the world in another way—by bringing healing to creation. We have the opportunity to witness with our hands, with our feet, and with the work that we do—rebuilding communities and eco-systems that are sustainable, and restoring relationship to all of God's creation.

QUESTIONS _____

1. Consider the most recent work project or trip in which you or your congregation participated. Did you think about how you could engage with that project or community long term? How would that have changed the work that was undertaken?
2. When your congregation responds to a natural disaster, does your entire congregation get involved? While members are on the trip, what would it look like for the rest of the congregation to be engaged in study about the region, and ways these kinds of natural disasters—or at least their worst impacts—could be prepared for or prevented?
3. In what ways does your congregation seek to live in better relationship with your community and environment?
4. The way humanity interacts with the environment is increasing the effects and frequency of natural disasters. What are two concrete steps you or your congregation can take to be involved in responding to that side of natural disasters?

13

When Disaster Hits Home

A Pastoral Response

We landed at the New Orleans airport mid-afternoon on April 29, 2010. I was a chaperone on my boys' choir tour—taking a rare Sunday off from preaching to accompany them on their trip. I had briefly been to New Orleans a few years before when our church helped in the disaster relief effort, and I was eager to see how the city had continued to recover from Hurricane Katrina.

That Saturday night, at the beginning of our concert at a large Baptist church, the host minister introduced us and then asked the congregation to pray for the flooding victims in Nashville. I had heard it was raining a lot back home—but I hadn't taken it too seriously. And now, here were the people of New Orleans, praying for flooding victims in Nashville. Weren't *we* supposed to be praying for *them*?

Sunday afternoon, as we heading to the airport to fly home, we got the word: Nashville's airport was closed. We couldn't fly home until Wednesday—sixty-six middle schoolers and twenty chaperones, all of us out of clean clothes. It didn't take much debate before we decided to charter two buses and drive back to Nashville. We spent Sunday night in a hotel, watching footage of the Nashville flood: row boats rescuing people from their houses, cars flipped upside down, school buildings floating

Jay Hartley is pastor of Eastwood Christian Church (DOC), in East Nashville, Tennessee, where he has served since 2000. During his tenure, ECC has been part of community rebuilding after a major tornado, and disaster relief following a major flood. He enjoys coaching little league baseball and waking church campers up by playing bagpipes.

down the interstate. A couple of choir members learned their houses were destroyed, but fortunately their families had made it to safety.

Monday afternoon, as we drove into Middle Tennessee, the skies were blue and the weather was perfect—just as it had been when we left four days before. As we neared downtown Nashville, water still covered the streets, parking lots, and several buildings visible from the interstate. But it was so peaceful. It was hard to believe Nashville had experienced such a natural disaster.

* * * * *

Disasters come in all shapes and sizes, and they call for different responses. Tornados, for example, leave dramatic destruction: trees blocking roads, homes reduced to toothpicks, cars smashed by trees. The need for immediate cleanup is obvious. Floods, on the other hand, are more subtle. Flooded homes are often ruined, but they don't always look so bad from the outside. They quickly develop mold, however, and everything that gets wet needs to be promptly removed.

But, in some ways, the pastoral response to a disaster requires the same steps as any pastoral response:

Inquire
Listen
Assess
Act, if possible.

Everybody reacts to tragedy differently, and everybody has different needs. The immediate aftermath of a disaster is like triage: Who needs immediate attention? Who needs financial help? A place to sleep? What about pets? Who has resources? Who doesn't? We have to inquire, listen, and assess any situation before we can act appropriately.

In some ways, I felt like an outsider, having been out of town during the two incessant days of rain, and fortunate that my house and church were for the most part unaffected. But again, the first pastoral response is to inquire. This first step can be the hardest. To call people who might be hurting, again and again, and hear their stories is never easy.

During my phone calls to check in with my congregation, I learned that two of our church families had lost their homes. One was taken care of by relatives and had no real need; the other was scrambling to find a place to stay and would be grateful for any help. Several families had flooded basements. Some had already taken care of the problem, but others needed help. In addition to the homeless family, the other critical need was a family with a flooded basement. Special equipment was needed to clean the basement, as the mother was pregnant and susceptible to health concerns caused by mold.

Having inquired and listened, we assessed the needs and assessed our resources. School was cancelled for the week, so our church youth group was available. And before I was even back in town, I had received messages from our denomination's disaster response fund, offering to help. Within a few days I had money to help the families in crisis.

Then it was time to act. Our youth group became a bucket brigade, helping haul damaged goods and buckets of water from several basements. The disaster ministry funds we received from our denomination were critical in helping the first family find shelter and helping the other family rent the masks and other special equipment necessary to clean their basement.

* * * * *

Curiously, one of my ongoing roles in response to the flood was as a community leader with the local Little League. What happens to children and youth while the adults are busy with additional cleanup responsibilities? Can you keep things as normal as possible for children? Should you? *Inquire, listen, assess, and act.*

Upon inquiry, we learned that our coaches and most families were not in immediate crisis. Our local Little League field, however, was completely ruined—and hundreds of fish were caught in the wire fencing. The concession stand and equipment shed were completely underwater, ruining everything: bases, balls, catchers' gear, mowers, grills, ice machines. There would be no way to play on those fields for the remaining six weeks of the season. But most parents were hoping the season could continue, as children were starting to go stir crazy and a sense of normalcy needed to be restored.

We decided to cancel the first week, because the entire community was scrambling and worrying about water shortages. But then we found some other, drier parks to use and made a completely new schedule. Within a week, children were back on the ball field, feeling like maybe life was getting back to normal. I recall the paralysis we felt after the terrorist attacks of 9/11—would life ever feel normal again? In our case, we chose to try to help the children get back to a routine as quickly as possible.

* * * * *

Perhaps the biggest learning for me during the Nashville floods was how helpful it is to have a close-knit, well-connected community. Ten years before the flood, our neighborhood had been hit by a massive tornado. After that disaster, churches, neighborhood organizations, and community groups had worked together and developed a network of relationships. That made all the difference. East Nashville has truly become a community—neighborhood leaders know each other and residents know they will support each other in times of crisis.

For instance, several neighborhood leaders have keys to our church building and know that, in a crisis, they can use our sanctuary and meeting spaces. Cases of water were delivered and stored in our sanctuary for emergency use after the flood. The neighborhood flood relief "command center" called a couple of times during the relief efforts: "We have some volunteers at a house and they have a situation where they need a pastor— can you come?" We have gotten to know and trust each other, enabling us to be an effective team.

Within 48 hours after the crest of the flood, over 250 homes in our neighborhood had been visited and surveyed. Volunteer crews stripped the damaged homes down to the studs—removing all wallboard, furniture, and debris. Because of that quick response, we avoided major mold problems. Neighbors cared for neighbors, and the need for very long-term disaster response was mitigated.

The lesson we learned was clear: the best way to prepare for an unforeseen disaster is to build relationships, establish a neighborhood network, and strengthen the local community's capacity to respond to those in need. All disasters are local. Perhaps the most critical work of a local faith leader or pastor is to connect, convene, organize, equip, and empower the local community to engage collaboratively in a pastoral response; to remind us that we're all in this together. For, as the apostle Paul points out in 1 Corinthians 12:26: when one member of the body suffers, everyone suffers. But when even one member is honored, we can all rejoice.

QUESTIONS

1. What sorts of relationships are most helpful for a pastoral staff to develop in a community to help prepare for a disaster?
2. What are the four steps of a pastoral response? Are they different during a disaster?
3. What needs might you anticipate in your community in the event of a disaster? What resources can you name that would help your community respond?

PROVIDING the EYE
in the STORM
Perspectives on Psychosocial Care
and Disaster Response

14

The Importance of Spiritual and Emotional Care

MARY HUGHES GAUDREAU

God is our refuge and strength,
a very present help in trouble.
Therefore we will not fear, though the earth should change,
though the mountains shake in the heart of the sea;
though its waters roar and foam,
though the mountains tremble with its tumult.
There is a river whose streams make glad the city of God,
the holy habitation of the Most High.
God is in the midst of the city; it shall not be moved;
God will help it when the morning dawns. (Psalm 46:1–5, NRSV)

Disasters bring to the surface some of our deepest and most challenging questions—questions about life, death, suffering, evil, meaning and purpose, and our connection to others: *Why did this happen to*

Mary Hughes Gaudreau is an ordained United Methodist deacon, licensed professional counselor, and disaster response specialist. A native of Oklahoma, she first entered into the disaster response field following the 1995 Oklahoma City Murrah Building bombing. Since that time she has provided direct training, response, and consultation in more than two dozen states affected by disasters, including the 1999 and 2003 Oklahoma tornado outbreaks, the 2004 Florida hurricanes, Hurricane Katrina and other Atlantic and Gulf Coast hurricanes, the 2011 Alabama tornadoes, Hurricane Sandy, and the Newtown, Connecticut (Sandy Hook), school shootings. She has served as a consultant for the United Methodist Committee on Relief since 2005 and designed UMCOR's national disaster spiritual and emotional Care Team program.

me? Why didn't this happen to me? Does anyone care about what has happened? Is there a Creator who cares? Where can I find hope? These are essentially theological and spiritual questions, and they are woven through the fabric of disaster recovery.

When disaster occurs, individuals and the whole community experience a wide range of losses. Beyond personal property, some face the loss of financial security, or familiar routines, or landmarks and neighborhoods. Others experience the loss of loved ones or the loss of their own health and well-being. The disorientation that accompanies these losses places tremendous pressure on personal, emotional, and spiritual strengths.

Disasters often amplify existing problems. They seems to find us *where we are most vulnerable* and they strike at the heart of our trust in ourselves and the world around us. As we tackle the details and challenges of rebuilding our lives, doubt or grief may lie just under the surface, breaking through the ways we keep ourselves busy. Often, this happens when we least expect it.

Individual reactions to the trauma and stress that accompany disasters vary from person to person. However, just as a community's overall disaster recovery often follows predictable patterns, emotional and spiritual needs also often follow predictable patterns. Simply understanding and recognizing the common spiritual and emotional responses to the challenges presented by disasters can provide comfort to those impacted. Eventually, many people are able to integrate their experiences with the disaster into their life experiences as a whole. As survivors move through grief, many begin to identify the overall timelines of their life stories with reference to the disaster—"before the tornado I worked at...," or "I remember because it was after the bombing and..."

Persons affected by disasters are often drawn to others with similar experiences, building a community of survivors who then offer support to those who may be just beginning a journey through disaster recovery.

- A number of Mississippi communities of faith affected by Hurricane Katrina have organized, trained, and mobilized early response teams to respond to disasters in their own state and beyond.
- Empowered through their own healing community and guided by a strong drive to provide hope and to "give back," individuals and families affected by the 1995 Oklahoma City Murrah Building bombing have regularly offered support to families affected by subsequent tragedies. Most recently, a group from Oklahoma City offered support to those affected by the 2013 Boston Marathon bombings.

Communities of Faith in Disaster Response

Local congregations, present before, during, and long after a disaster event, are uniquely positioned to provide spiritual and emotional care for those within their congregations and for the larger community. When people of faith respond to any disaster-related need, their compassionate presence and acts of caring contain underlying or *intrinsic* spiritual care. Experienced faith-based disaster response leaders will often remark, "Everything we do *is* spiritual care."

Faith communities also provide *intentional* or specific spiritual care as a part of regular congregational life. Such gestures of *intentional* spiritual care provide a sense of safety and stability to those impacted by disasters. Examples of intentional spiritual care include familiar liturgy, ritual, commemorative services, music, appropriate pastoral care and prayer, sermons, structured support group activities, educational events, and other ministries. When adapted and extended in response to a new, post-disaster reality, these *intentional* spiritual care activities counter the hopelessness that often accompanies disaster.

Following the horrific school shootings at Sandy Hook Elementary School in Newtown, Connecticut, Newtown United Methodist Church found itself at the center of a community trying to make sense of incomprehensible sorrow. Just blocks from the school and the spontaneous memorial that tens of thousands of visitors had created, the church opened its sanctuary as a protected, quiet refuge away from the crowds and the intense gaze of the media. The church's very existence in the community, their proximity to the event, and their willingness to simply be present provided a type of extemporaneous intrinsic spiritual care.

Though quite vulnerable themselves, Newtown church members also provided types of intentional spiritual care. Prayer and pastoral conversation were available to members and guests at their request. Regular services included liturgy, prayers, sermons, and music that had been adapted to the context of the tragedy. One week after the shootings, the congregation participated in a community-wide day of remembrance. Gathered in the sanctuary, members of the church and members of the wider community joined other local faith communities in ringing their steeple bells in memory of those lost. Immediately following the ringing of the bells the congregation again stepped outside for prayers, singing, and words of hope and healing.

With this understanding as a foundation, how might local communities of faith prepare to address spiritual and emotional care needs following disasters?

Educate Yourself about the Needs and How to Best Respond

- Post-disaster spiritual and emotional care needs present unique challenges. Many faith-based disaster response organizations, especially those affiliated with National Voluntary Organizations Active in Disaster (National VOAD), provide excellent training and consultation regarding spiritual and emotional care following a disaster. The National VOAD Emotional and Spiritual Care Committee addresses existing and emerging disaster-related spiritual and emotional care issues. Through this committee, National VOAD has established resources, ethical standards, and other guidance regarding disaster spiritual and emotional care. National VOAD's *Light Our Way, a Guide for Spiritual Care in Times of Disaster* is designed for disaster response volunteers, first responders, and disaster recovery specialists. The National VOAD Spiritual Care "Points of Consensus" document outlines specific standards for disaster spiritual care providers.[1] *Include spiritual and emotional care in your disaster response planning.*

- Reading this material is an important step in preparing for disasters that might strike your community. Individuals, families, and congregations who have prepared for disaster are more able to respond productively and creatively to the broad ranging needs that emerge following disasters.

- Because of their role in providing a stabilizing sense of safety to their communities, congregations are encouraged to quickly re-establish some regular activities. Plan to hold worship services and other gatherings as soon as possible, even if those must be held in an alternative location.

- Consider how you might change or extend existing ministries to address post-disaster needs.

Get Connected

- Connect with others in your community and beyond who can assist in your spiritual and emotional care planning and activities. Know that a broad network of state, denominational, and national organizations can offer assistance and guidance. Primary connections include your local ministerial association, your state Voluntary Organizations Active in Disaster (VOAD), and National VOAD.

- Learn your referral resources. Spiritual care is best offered alongside a strong network of agencies to which you can refer people for disaster-related needs such as food, clothing, shelter, health, and transportation. Be prepared to refer them to appropriate mental/behavioral health resources as well.

Remember Long-Term Needs

• Many disaster plans focus on the days and weeks following a disaster. Prepared congregations know that full recovery takes much longer. Some individuals and families will be able to return to their normal routine quickly. For others, the process of recovery may take much longer. Those impacted by disaster will delay addressing their spiritual and emotional care needs until basic needs (food, clothing, and shelter) are met. It is critical to be aware of spiritual and emotional care needs that emerge long after the attention of news media has turned elsewhere. Compassionate and wise congregations understand the long-term nature of disaster recovery. By clearly communicating this through both words and actions, they provide healing and hope to those who might otherwise feel forgotten or misunderstood.

Know Your Strengths; Know Your Limits

• Local communities of faith are uniquely gifted in providing healing care. Seasoned disaster response veterans often remark that *all disasters are local*. Some disasters, however, require support from outside the impacted community. Examples may include disasters that overwhelm the capacity of local providers, disasters receiving a great deal of media attention, disasters that require controlled access, disasters resulting in mass casualties, and disaster-related settings in which people from diverse faith backgrounds will request spiritual care.
• Self-care is a significant spiritual and emotional care concern for those responding as well as for those directly impacted by disasters. Responding to overwhelming disaster-related needs is exhausting. Be prepared to address the long-term emotional and spiritual fatigue that naturally results from this work.

Recovering from a disaster includes physical, material, and financial recovery. It necessarily includes the often deep-seated and powerful needs of emotional and spiritual health. Faith communities are uniquely positioned and have a strong influence on individuals' and communities' spiritual and emotional well-being. To provide care and support is, in essence, one of the most fundamental roles of a local faith community. To do this after a disaster is only natural. But, to do it well, congregations are wise to prepare by sharpening their best practices in spiritual and emotional care on a regular basis.

As people of faith who both experience and respond to disasters, we can draw upon strength and courage beyond our own imaginations. In doing so, we kindle hope, resilience, and healing.

RESOURCES

Baird, Rebecca. *Leslie Weatherhead's The Will of God Workbook.* Nashville: Abingdon, 1995.

Community Arise: A Disaster Ministry Curriculum—http://www. communityarise.com/

Light Our Way: A Guide for Spiritual Care in Times of Disaster for Disaster Response Volunteers, First Responders and Disaster Planners— http://www.nvoadstore.com/light-our-way.html

Herman, Judith. *Trauma and Recovery: The Aftermath of Violence—from Domestic Abuse to Political Terror.* New York: BasicBooks, 1997.

The National Child Traumatic Stress Network—http://www.nctsnet.org

National Voluntary Organizations Active in Disaster—www.nvoad.org

National Voluntary Organizations Active in Disaster Points of Consensus (Disaster Spiritual Care)—http://www.nvoad.org/index. php?option=com_jdownloads&Itemid=41&view=viewdownload&c atid=4&cid=16

Weatherhead, Leslie D. *The Will of God.* Nashville: Abingdon, 1944.

QUESTIONS

1. Read the National Voluntary Organizations Active in Disaster "Points of Consensus for Disaster Spiritual Care." These standards for disaster spiritual care are agreed upon by all members of National VOAD. What do you think of these standards?
2. What circumstances have you seen that cause spiritual care following disasters to be different from spiritual care provided in nondisaster times?
3. What existing ministries within your congregation might be adapted or extended to address spiritual care for your community after a disaster?
4. What are three "next steps" you or your community of faith can take to connect with the larger disaster spiritual care community?

15

What Faith Communities Need to Know

An Evidence-based Approach to Stress and Trauma Care

LISA HALE

"In your desperation, you opened your heart in prayer, and what happened? You didn't get a miracle to avert a tragedy. But you discovered people around you, and God beside you, and strength within you to help you survive the tragedy. I offer that as an example of a prayer being answered."[1]

—HAROLD KUSHNER

Following immediate needs for rescue, safety, sustenance, and shelter, a broader response to a traumatic event is shaped by the religious, ethnic, and cultural beliefs of a community. As with the repair of buildings and ongoing replenishment of goods, healing from physical injuries and emotional aftermath is a gradual process. There are lingering reactions to experiencing a disaster; for many, high levels of fear, anxiety, and stress may contribute to the disaster's impact on their lives in the days and months following an event. It is not uncommon for people to find

Lisa R. Hale holds a Ph.D. in clinical and health psychology and is director of the Kansas City Center for Anxiety Treatment and an Adjunct Associate Professor of Psychology at the University of Missouri-Kansas City. Dr. Hale receives research funding from the National Institute of Mental Health, has served on the Board of Directors for the Anxiety and Depression Association of America, and provides presentations, consulting services and outreach programing to organizations and media sources at local and national levels.

themselves unable to stop replaying what happened for an extended period of time. And while such memories stay with us, becoming part of our personal stories and the history of a community, a majority of individuals will naturally adapt. Resources within the human mind and body are known to prevail when faced with changes in circumstance; meeting the needs of basic daily living seems to move us forward in finding a renewed and meaningful life path. Religious practices are part of this process for many, having been noted in some studies as the predominant method of coping with a stressful event for over 50 percent of individuals.[2]

An inherent strength of faith communities is in promoting healing, acceptance, and hope—a challenging role when circumstances are darkest or healing does not occur as hoped.

A Starting Path

The most helpful framework for considering mental health needs immediately post-incident requires recognizing that, for most people, emotional recovery will come naturally over time, aided by strengths inherent to human nature and social support. That said, it is equally important to remain aware of potential signs that a person has been more significantly impacted—with ongoing interference in areas of relationships, work/education, or other life activities—and in need of appropriate professional intervention. Given that people are five times more likely to seek out clergy during times of crisis than all other forms of mental health resources or support combined,[3] religious communities bear an important front-line responsibility for directing to, understanding of, and providing access to the types of activities and information most likely to be of help.

Following extensive scientific review and conferences held for developing expert guidelines, the National Institute of Mental Health (NIMH) has promoted a model of disaster "first aid" response that is parallel to traditional medical intervention. Namely, both types of first aid include stabilization of the patient, reduction of harm, then referral as needed to more advanced care.[4] Faith communities are ideally suited to many of the practical, hands-on support objectives of Psychological First Aid (PFA), including mobilizing support for the distressed, helping reunite and keep families together, and communicating information and education.[5] Further, it is notable that research findings of traits which support effective outcomes in PFA delivery closely match those qualities of established religious homes, namely: developing a sense of safety; calming; connectedness to others; sense of efficacy for self and community; and hopefulness.[6]

One of the most salient and useful roles of religious communities during the aftermath of a disaster is in the capabilities of connecting people—to each other, and to quality information. Creating a plan for developing a resource structure of ongoing opportunities for gatherings (both informational meetings and support groups may be useful), networking to emergency channels, and sharing educational and resource information may be ideally promoted through a variety of methods. Websites, social media, fliers, public service announcements, and even community canvassing may be beneficial in order to ensure reaching the broadest segments of those possibly affected. Ongoing and repetitive timing of these activities is important, too, since when emotional arousal and physical/base levels of human need is high (as in the immediate periods that follow a traumatic event) people may have difficulty learning and remembering new information.

A Wide Range of Normal

A desire to aid others can be particularly powerful in post-disaster periods; it may be one of the rare times that communities find themselves overwhelmed with offers to volunteer. While such generosity is encouraged and welcomed, some caution must be used when approaching plans for training, collecting materials, and considering program development. Appointing a central committee (whether internal to a denomination and/ or connecting a number of different religious homes in the community) can aid in efficient review and decision making, helping avoid haphazard efforts or overlaps in leadership. Information used should be derived from credible resources (and then fact-checked) to diminish a spread of misinformation, which easily occurs in times of crisis. Volunteers working directly with the public should be provided basic education about the vast array of reactions people might have following traumatic events. For example, while people often can intuitively understand strong emotional displays, aid workers should also be prepped to meet those with calmer or more private coping styles. Those individuals can experience guilt or "reverse stigmatization"—e.g., if they don't exhibit certain symptoms, they may be carelessly labeled as "less feeling."[7]

Additionally, direct, tangible activities of program efforts should not extend beyond the realistic scope and qualifications of its volunteers. An ideal emphasis for religious communities often remains in building resiliency facilitated by social support: through the caring and trusted presence of spiritual connections, the most applicable information and services can be collected and linked to those in need. The designated central committee and religious leadership can monitor for difficulties that may arise, or the detection of any areas of need that appear unmet.

Encountering Greater Need

While no hard and fast timetables exist, individuals not exhibiting significant symptom levels two months post-event are typically not considered in need of ongoing mental health monitoring or follow up, unless they specifically request it.[8] There may be certain groups warranting additional monitoring and attention of community outreach and resources. These would include individuals having pre-existing difficulties with anxiety, depression, or other mental health disorders, whereby the incident may increase baseline symptoms and place them at particular risk for developing adjustment difficulties to the event. Other individuals and groups who may also be considered for further attention would include the bereaved, individuals who had required significant medical attention from the event, and those whose exposure had been particularly extended in duration or intensity. Children and elderly populations may also display particular needs for reassurance of their health and safety, and their families may require additional support and assistance in finding appropriate ways to communicate this.

For those individuals who do exhibit ongoing distress and life interference, sorting through the maze of healthcare information can be a daunting task. There are two forms of supported intervention for trauma and acute stress-related disorders—medication and specifically targeted psychotherapies. These are either used separately or combined, dependent on a number of factors that may include symptom severity, age, other health conditions, and patient preference. A type of treatment called Cognitive Behavioral Therapies (CBT) has derived the most scientific evidence and consistent support in expert clinical practice guidelines, with adaptations across all age groups. These treatments specifically aim to modify relationships between thoughts, feelings, and behaviors that impact symptoms, and promote effective processing of emotional and cognitive memory functions. Primary examples include Prolonged Exposure Therapy (PE), Cognitive Processing Therapy (CPT), and Trauma-Focused Cognitive-Behavioral Therapy for children. Unfortunately, the largest downside to CBT therapies is that it can be difficult to locate a well-trained provider in many communities (more on that later).

Medication treatment for acute traumatic stress reactions (within one month of the event) would generally only be recommended for those with clinically interfering symptoms that have been unresponsive to a brief individual or group psychotherapy intervention. The evidence base is strongest for the selective serotonin reuptake inhibitors (SSRIs), with sertraline (brand name Zoloft) and paroxetine (Paxil) FDA approved for treating PTSD in adults.[9] Currently, none are approved for the treatment of PTSD in the pediatric population. Although studies have not shown benzodiazepine medications to be useful in targeting core PTSD symptoms, in some instances their short-term use may be indicated for targeting symptoms of extreme arousal, insomnia, and anxiety (examples include Lorazepam [Ativan] and Alprazolam [Xanax]). However, this medication class must be used with caution due to its high addiction properties and possible interference with cognitive processes, including those implicated in successful response to psychotherapy.[10] On an individual basis, there may be other useful medications to consider; working closely with a primary care physician, and, as needed, a psychiatry specialist, is the best approach when considering pharmacological care.

The Critical Healthcare Consumer: What Works

An unfortunate reality when seeking services is the amount of questionable practices one may encounter—in many cases, simply unhelpful; in worst cases, potentially harmful. Due to the fact almost anything may be labeled "therapeutic" without consequence, there is a need to explicitly search for treatments that are evidence-based and delivered by a credibly trained provider. At minimum, clinicians should have a graduate-level or doctoral degree and be licensed in their state or country. Typically they will hold internship or residency training, and past supervised experience in the specific treatment technique or approach used. For the treatment of children or adolescents, the provider should have specific training with these populations.

Despite having the most evidence-based support for effectiveness, CBT therapies are unfortunately less commonly used in community practice. Therefore, as mentioned earlier, it may be more difficult to locate a qualified provider. Providing in resource materials weblinks and listings of recognized mental health organizations for education about supported treatments may be additionally beneficial in that many also provide "find a therapist" services and/or guidelines of questions one should ask when interviewing potential therapists. In some cases it may be worthwhile and most efficient to seek an expert opinion at a nationally recognized clinic, medical center, or university program, even if one must travel outside the local area. Many medical and/or therapy specialists are able to serve as consultants, coordinating either portions of treatment or aftercare with more local providers.

It is also helpful to remain aware that some commonly held perceptions and treatment practices may continue to exist in spite of scientific refute. For example, providing Critical Incidence Stress Debriefing to all experiencing a traumatic event in attempts to prevent later psychological difficulties is considered largely ineffective as well as potentially harmful for some participants.[11] More recently, however, promising early intervention research using focused adaptations of established exposure-based therapies showed effectiveness when delivered as soon as eleven to twelve hours post severe traumatic event.[12] Unfortunately, fad approaches also readily arise in the mental health field gaining enthusiasm with exaggerated promises of "easier, faster, better" results. Notable examples would be steering patients toward neurofeedback over first-line approaches, or suggestions that current brain scan technologies are helpful in the individual treatment of psychiatric disorders (both overstating the current science).[13] Any claims of "a cure" or "revolutionary" treatment should also be met with healthy suspicion.

One area of longstanding controversy in the field of trauma treatment has been that of Eye Movement Desensitization and Reprocessing Therapy (EMDR). EMDR uses components of CBT paired with specific eye movements (or in some cases, rhythmic movements such as tapping) that are purported to assist brain processes. Improvements in research methods from earlier EMDR studies have recently led most (but not all) practice guidelines to list it as an evidence-based treatment at least for PTSD in adults.[14] Still, many original questions pertaining to its practice are unresolved.[15] A main scientific critique remains in that therapeutic improvement in EMDR appears tied to tenets of basic exposure therapy, and a lack of evidence that the eye-movement or tapping components add anything beyond basic CBT. As a result, EMDR may be thought to resemble a diluted form of exposure therapy, yet there is no evidence to support its proponents considering it a treatment of choice over other cognitive behavioral approaches. Additional criticisms of EMDR have arisen from clinicians widely extending its application to an array of unsupported or untested other clinical conditions.

Patients and their advocates are encouraged to reach out for assistance in locating providers, to ask lots of questions, and to request solid references for *any* suggested treatment. Families of those reluctant to seek help may find it helpful to begin initial discussions with a trusted family physician or clergy member. As emphasized previously, obtaining the most helpful guidance may sometimes mean seeking referrals from and/or consulting with a provider holding a background of both clinical and research training focused on anxiety disorders. In taking these steps, families can be helped to reach a position where they can confidently weigh and understand the individual options that may be right for them.

Equally important to promoting successful outreach and outcomes would be continued efforts at better equipping the helping professionals themselves—religious leaders and mental health providers—to collaborate. While pastoral counseling is an expected and customary role, religious leaders have very limited exposure to evidence-based treatments for psychopathology or skills for assessing referral sources.[16]

Likewise, mental health professionals may not readily identify areas where a lack of awareness of religious or cultural norms may impede treatment, or where involving elements of religious life may better inform intervention.[17] Communities not already doing so may wish to consider these issues when forming resource or long-term recovery committees or task forces.

Final Notes

An extensive discussion of trauma treatment is beyond the scope or purpose of this essay. Readers are referred to the Treatment Guidelines available through either the website of the International Society for Traumatic Stress Studies (ISTSS; http://www.istss.org/TreatmentGuidelines/4579. htm) or included within the book *Effective Treatments for PTSD*, Second Edition.[18] Information provided here is a broad educational overview. Always speak with your provider about individual clinical needs.

> "We need to get over the questions that focus on the past and on the pain—'Why did this happen to me' and ask instead the question which opens the doors for the future, 'Now that this has happened, what shall I do about it?'" —KUSHNER [19]

RESOURCES FOR FURTHER INFORMATION _____

International Society for Traumatic Stress Studies (ISTSS)
   http://www.istss.org
Anxiety and Depression Association of America (ADAA)
   http://www.adaa.org
Association for Behavioral and Cognitive Therapies (ABCT)
   http://abct.org
National Institute of Mental Health
   http://www.nimh.nih.gov/health/topics/coping-with-traumatic-events/index.shtml
Centers for Disease Control and Prevention
   http://www.bt.cdc.gov/masscasualties/copingpub.asp
Center for Disaster and Extreme Event Preparedness (DEEP Center) http://www.umdeepcenter.org/

QUESTIONS _____

1. What mental health resources are available in your community?
2. What does "evidence-based" mental health care mean? Why is it important?
3. What ways does your congregation help people build community?
4. If a person in your congregation showed signs of PTSD following a disaster, would you know how to help them find appropriate care? What systems does your church have in place?

16

Ensuring Resiliency in Children after a Disaster

JUDY BEZON-BRAUNE

When a television reporter puts together a news story following a disaster, it's not unusual to seek out stories that carry emotional weight. It's easy to look at children playing and think, as most people do, that children are carefree and fortunate to be resilient and oblivious to the dire consequences of the disaster's destruction. A film clip of children playing would make a good contrast to interviews with distraught survivors.

Unfortunately, this would be an incorrect assumption. Children are deeply impacted by disasters, but lack the words and concepts to express themselves. Play is their method of communication. It is how they explore their concerns and come to grips with realities they do not understand. When you understand this and interact with a child playing after experiencing a disaster, you'll find that often the play is disaster-related.

The kids who are running around playing tag or kicking a ball? They have found a way to dissipate nervous tension and anxiety through exercise. Focusing on the game distracts children from worries and concerns that will return soon after they stop.

The children who are playing with blocks or a tool kit? Is that idle play, or could they be emulating all they see around them as the community

Judy Bezon-Braune was the associate director for Children's Disaster Services (CDS) from September 2007–December 2012. Her responsibilities included program development and expansion; supervision of staff; training, certification, and deployment of volunteers; managing inter-agency relations; and creating partnerships to expand the capacity of the rapid response program.

cleans up and rebuilds? It is possible that they are, in their own way, trying to contribute to the recovery of their family or community?

And what about the child playing quietly with dolls? If you listen while he or she plays, you might find that as he or she puts the baby doll to bed, the baby has been protected so it will not be impacted by another disaster. The baby bed might then be placed on a stack of blocks "to stay high out of the water," the child might explain.

What about the brother and sister playing with cardboard boxes? Listening to them you learn that *this* house they are building will be tornado-(disaster)-proof.

Despite what adults often perceive, children are deeply impacted by disasters, and they are impacted differently than adults. Children wonder if the disaster will happen again. They worry that someone they love will be hurt. As they imagine the future, they wonder who will take care of them if something happens to their parents. These concerns are experienced as upsetting feelings rather than specific fears they can articulate. Children usually do not have the language or understanding of their feelings to communicate their concerns. They do not have experience to know that sharing a worry will help them feel better. They do not have the perspective from past events that, over time, things will get better.

Because their play is misinterpreted by adults as fun and carefree, children's needs are often not recognized or addressed. With most of the adults around them in survival/recovery mode with numerous anxiety-provoking tasks to tend to (Are the relatives okay? Where will we live? Do I have a job? How will we eat?), it is easy to see how children's needs and concerns are not always recognized or addressed.

So how do we help the littlest survivors?

Infants and Toddlers

Infants pick up on the tension and anxiety of the people around them. They may not be aware of the events of the disaster, but they are acutely aware of the emotional state of their caregivers and can be fussy when those around them are tense and upset. Parents and caregivers should use a calm, reassuring tone of voice and as much as possible keep to predisaster routines for feeding and sleeping. Hold and cuddle them often, using familiar words or songs. Keep comfort items such as a favorite stuffed animal or blanket near, and if they are not available, try to replace them with something similar.

Toddlers (1–2 years old) can see the disruption around them, but do not understand what is happening. They, too gain security from routine, so re-establishing their schedule will help them readjust. Eating, naps, play, and quiet times should be kept as routine as possible. Comfort items such as a favorite toy or blanket, stuffed animal or book are important at this age, as are bedtime or mealtime rituals (a story before bed, tucking in, grace before meals, etc.).

As with infants, this age group also benefits from frequent holding and cuddling. Soothing words are helpful and may need to be repeated often for reassurance. Physical activities might help them "blow off steam" and make it easier to nap in unfamiliar settings. Simple explanations of what has happened and plans for recovery should be used as appropriate. Address concerns as they are expressed. Reflecting back a toddler's feelings may help the child begin to understand his or her emotions. Having feelings recognized will help the toddler to feel understood, increasing the child's sense of security.

Preschool and Early Elementary

Preschool and early elementary children are observing and learning all the time. They learn from watching the adults around them, and subsequently try to act like them. This makes it very important for adults to monitor their reactions to the disaster and to be as optimistic as possible. This is not to say that adults should deny concern or worry. Children read tense body language well. An insincere or forced statement, such as "There's nothing to worry about. Everything will be okay," will not ring true.

Limiting exposure to television coverage of the disaster is crucial for children. I recall a young girl who, upon seeing repeated images of planes crashing into the World Trade Center, desperately asked "Mommy, why don't they make them stop?" Seeing the disaster replayed on television, children may think the destruction of the disaster is continuing. It is best that they are not exposed to the drama and sensationalism of seeing the worst of the disaster played over and over again. We can avoid frightening them further by turning the television off.

However, honesty is important. Parents and caregivers will be tense and worried about the future. It is important to answer questions honestly, but with an upbeat tone. If there is something you don't know, it is better to say so than to lie. For example, respond with "I'm sure things will get better. We're just not sure how that will happen, but we'll keep working on it"

At this age, too, a sense of routine contributes to a child's security. Bedtime and mealtime rituals contribute to a sense of continuity—*"My family is the same, even though everything else seems different."* Getting children back in day care, preschool, or school is part of re-establishing their routine. As soon as those resources are available, it's important to return to that part of the child's routine, even if it means enrolling in a new school.

Consider explaining this change by telling a child, "Yes, we're worried about where we're going to live, but we'll figure it out. There are people who can help us."

Play is important to a child after a disaster. Getting together with peers or friends can be comforting. Playing with toys is a familiar and comforting activity, restoring a bit of normalcy to their experience.

Some toys are "scripted," and have a specific way to be used—dolls or "action figures" based on television characters have a set way to be played with, as determined by the television show's plot. Other toys are unscripted and do not have any one set way to be used. When children play with toys like this, their play tends to bring out whatever is on their minds, and allows them to explore their experiences and feelings. This makes toys such as paints, crayons, markers, puppets, baby dolls, dress-up clothes, blocks, cars, a doctor kit, or a tool kit ideal for play after a disaster.

Using imagination, a child can explore her or his experience of the disaster through play. An adult with a listening ear who plays with the child and allows the child to lead the play can help the child sort through his or her reactions to the disaster events. As the adult does this, the child feels understood and will express him- or herself further, more able to explore feelings and the experience of the disaster.

Adults should reflect what they see and hear in a child's play—both concerning the play itself and the feelings the child seems to express. For example, if a child is packing things to evacuate, an adult might say, "You have to leave, and are making sure to take everything you need." If the child seems frantic as he or she plays through this, the adult might say, "You seem worried about getting things packed in time." If other children are building with blocks, the adult might comment on what they are building. If the blocks fall down, the adult might reflect that they put a lot of work into building and now it has fallen down, asking them, "I wonder if that makes you feel sad or mad?" It is this type of interaction— an adult understanding and accepting how the child feels—that can help the child begin to understand his or her experience of the disaster and move forward.

Upper Elementary Children

As children approach the upper elementary grades, all of the above suggestions are appropriate to use. Protect them from sensationalized coverage of the disaster by the media. Playing with toys that require imagination—art materials, blocks, dolls, medical kits, tool kits, etc.— remains an excellent activity for older elementary children, who will also benefit from time with friends and a chance to share their experiences.

Playing a simple game with an adult is another way to engage with children of this age. The game provides structure or a "reason" for being together. While they play, there will be discussion about the game. If the game does not require a great deal of thought or strategy, such as Sorry or Uno, then other topics may emerge.

Also helpful are group games, opportunities for movement, and exercise with peers and friends. Playing a simple game, running an errand, or helping a trusted adult with a chore may provide time to talk while being active and engaged.

Making time to talk with a child in this way is very important after a disaster. While engaged in another activity, a child might begin discussing his or her experiences without being asked. At this point it is important to let the child lead the discussion, instead of sharing one's own experiences, thoughts, and feelings. Adults should reflect what that they hear, making sure to include both the child's experiences and the feelings that seem to be behind those experiences, while leaving room for the child to correct what's been reflected. (*"You saw the water in the yard and that was confusing, because you'd never seen water there."*) An adult only needs to reflect what has been said and the child will continue to share his or her experiences. Probing questions should be avoided, as they could easily take the child beyond his or her comfort zone. The child could become anxious, stop talking, or change the topic.

The only exception to the adult going beyond simply reflecting back what he or she hears in the child's experiences would be if rumors or misperceptions are voiced by the child, at which point correct information should be gently given. Simple, clear, and honest explanations are always best.

Teens

In many ways, teenagers are somewhere between being a child and being a grown up. They face higher expectations for behavior and maturity, but retain a strong desire to have fun and play. While it would be a mistake to treat them as children, it would also be a mistake to assume they will cope with adult maturity.

Teens want to be noticed, need to be appreciated, and have a desire to make a difference in the world. Teens have a strong desire to spend time with their peers, fit in, and be accepted. These needs do not change after a disaster, but they may no longer be able to get together with friends, leaving them feeling isolated and adrift.

It is important for teens to have opportunities to get together with peers to "hang out." This gives them a chance to discuss their experiences, find support from one another, and discover that they are not alone in feeling the way they do. Physical activities are also important as a way to release pent up energy—a basketball game or other game will help them stay active.

If there are teens in your family, it is tempting to use them as confidants or rely on them too much for help. This should be avoided, as they are not yet ready to assume the roles of adult friends. They can and should help the family, but should not be required or expected to take on adult responsibilities.

Teenagers can contribute to a community's recovery in real and tangible ways, however, and for them to do so is a great way to help teens recover from the trauma of a disaster. Contributing to a community's recovery in safe, age-appropriate ways can be a life-changing experience for a young person. Teens might work with adults to cart away brush and downed limbs, check health kits for distribution, or perform other basic cleanup tasks. With proper instruction, they can help rebuild damaged homes. They can join just about any group that is engaged in tasks that are needed for recovery. This is especially helpful if teens can work in a group, because being with their peers helps meet their social needs and allows them to make a meaningful contribution.

But it is important that the work teens do is not unnecessary "busy work." For example, sweeping a parking lot to remove nails that would puncture tires is necessary work. Someone has to do it so cars will not be damaged. Sweeping a parking lot because there are plenty of brooms and the teens would be kept busy is not essential and will be seen for what it is. Look at what needs to be done in the community and find a way to integrate teenagers into the list. Feeding large groups of people? Signing in people as they pick up donated items? Teens can make a significant contribution, given proper supervision and guidance.

Whether it is helping young children find ways to play and release tension following a disaster, providing age-appropriate answers for the questions children raise in the midst of recovery, or facilitating ways teenagers might contribute to rebuilding the community that has nurtured them, children of all ages have significant needs following disasters. As communities of faith come together to provide care for a community post-disaster, it is critical that children and teens do not get lost in the shuffle.

QUESTIONS _____

1. What have you observed when you've seen children play? What are your assumptions when you see children playing outside? When you see them playing with toys?

2. How is play with "scripted toys" different from play with toys that promote imaginative play? Why would toys that promote imaginative play be particularly helpful to a child after an upsetting experience?

3. How can your church community support families with children after a disaster? (Consider each age group—infants, toddlers, preschool, early elementary, later elementary, teens.)

4. Teens are less likely to play with toys. What materials or activities can be used to bring up what is on their minds? What are the potential disasters that might impact our community? Thinking of that type of disaster(s)—Which tasks would need to be done that teens could perform?

17

"Hurt People Hurt Other People"

A Trauma-Sensitive Disaster Response Model

ELAINE ZOOK BARGE

In a conversation about ten years ago with disaster response specialists based in Central America, the team leader told us that they know very well how to provide access to food and potable water; restore basic services such as medical care and electricity; and reconstruct houses, bridges, and roads. But, in the evenings when they sit with people from the affected population, they do not know what to say or how to engage in conversation. This organization, like many other humanitarian aid and development agencies, did not have a trauma-sensitive framework that included the creation of social space for sharing stories to help heal fears and wounds as part of its "reconstruction" response, or staff with training and confidence to facilitate such a space.

Earthquakes, tsunamis, floods, hurricanes, and wars all greatly affect communities and individuals. When disaster of any type strikes, it creates chaos, turmoil, confusion, great uncertainty, and fear as people look to the future as well as how they will cope and survive in the present. Community and individual resilience is sorely tested. Everyone, both the

---

Elaine Zook Barge is the director of strategies for trauma awareness and resilience (STAR), an evidence-based training program for those whose work brings them in contact with populations dealing with historic or current trauma. During the 1980s and 1990s she worked in El Salvador, Nicaragua, and Guatemala with Mennonite Central Committee. In her work with communities in conflict zones, she observed firsthand war, poverty, displacement, and resilience, and would have welcomed a resource such as STAR in order to be more trauma-informed. She currently facilitates STAR trainings at Eastern Mennonite University, throughout the U.S., and in Africa, Asia, Latin America, and the Caribbean.

affected population as well as the crisis responders, experiences extreme stress; some to the point of being overwhelmed, thus producing short- or long-term trauma. Organizations typically enter as emergency responders and eventually move on or are replaced by organizations committed to reconstruction and development or economic recovery. A trauma-sensitive framework is needed at each stage of disaster response.

Nicaraguan psychologist Martha Cabrera noted the need for a more comprehensive emergency response framework in 1998 following Hurricane Mitch when she and her colleagues traveled to the affected regions of Nicaragua with a goal of addressing psychological needs. They were surprised that no one seemed to be taking into account the emotional, psychological, or spiritual needs of the people. They realized that Nicaragua, recovering from not only a natural disaster but longstanding civil conflict, was a "multiply wounded country,"[1] as they found high levels of apathy, isolation, aggressiveness, abuse, and chronic illness; and low levels of flexibility, tolerance, and the ability to trust and work together. Cabrera concluded that it is hard to move forward when the personal and communal history still hurts.[2]

Carolyn Yoder, founding director of Strategies for Trauma Awareness and Resilience (STAR), notes that what Cabrera and team discovered are the effects of trauma on the body, brain, and behavior of individuals, communities, and societies. While some humanitarian and development organizations are beginning to include psychosocial programs with populations who have experienced natural disasters or violence, Yoder recommends that "organizations become 'trauma-informed' so that a trauma-sensitive framework can be integrated into any project: economic, health, governance, and others. This means more than putting a psychologist on every project team. Awareness of the repercussions of trauma needs to extend across the organization, to headquarters and field staff alike".[3]

Yoder further explains that being trauma-informed includes the following: [4]

- Understanding the physiological, emotional, cognitive, behavioral, and spiritual impact of traumatic events (current or historic) on recipient populations, and how unaddressed trauma contributes to cycles of violence.
- Recognizing community and societal dynamics and behaviors that are indicators of unaddressed trauma.
- Identifying processes from multiple fields—human security (including economic security), conflict transformation, restorative

justice, neurobiology, psychology, and spirituality—that can be integrated to address trauma and increase resilience.

- Recognizing that addressing the psychological needs of populations creates the need to monitor staff for secondary trauma and to equip them with self-care skills and tools.

Many leaders, caregivers, and practitioners have become more trauma-informed during the past twelve years through the Strategies for Trauma Awareness and Resilience (STAR) program at Eastern Mennonite University (EMU). In collaboration with Church World Service (CWS), EMU developed an integrated multidisciplinary approach to respond to disasters in ways that take trauma and resilience seriously in the wake of the traumatic events of September 11, 2001. This approach considers the effects of trauma on the body, brain, behavior, and beliefs and recognizes that short-term and long-term responses need to include consideration of trauma's varying effects on communities and caregivers. STAR's conceptual framework brings together knowledge and practices derived from neurobiology, conflict transformation, human security, spirituality, and restorative justice. This integrated framework helps individuals and communities normalize responses to trauma-producing events and understand the link between unhealed trauma and cycles of violence—hurting ourselves or others. They leave with tools and processes for addressing trauma, breaking cycles of violence, and building resilience—tools for helping others and themselves.

The responses to traumatic events are different for everyone, and it is important to remember that not everyone who experiences a traumatic event or situation experiences trauma. Understanding this makes us gentler with ourselves and less judgmental of others. Trauma impacts individuals and groups longer-term in ways that can be observed physically, emotionally, spiritually, and in the way we think (cognitively) and behave. A list of common trauma reactions can be found on the STAR web page at http://www.emu.edu/cjp/star/toolkit/normal-reactions.pdf , with a broader description of the impact of trauma on the body, brain, behavior, and beliefs in the following section.[5]

Trauma and the Body

When faced with threat or danger, the body quickly gets ready for action by producing an enormous amount of energy, which is released in the "fight or flight" response. The freeze response, on the other hand, traps the fight/flight energy in the nervous system and muscles and, if not released, can stay trapped in the body in the form of stress or trauma reactions. Peter Levine, a psychologist and biophysicist who has worked in the field of stress and trauma for more than forty years, has studied wild animals and discovered that they do not exhibit long-term trauma responses or PTSD like humans because their instinctual responses of trembling, shaking, deep breathing, and panting release the energy. Shaking, trembling, crying, and sweating are also normal responses for humans and are all good signs, according to Levine. "This means that we are discharging some of the energy and the body is regaining its balance. You want to allow what's happening in the body to happen without interference or judgment. Just watch and understand that the human body has the innate ability to regain its balance if we just let it feel what it feels and give it time to do what it needs to do. This is how we 'resolve' trauma before it takes hold."[6] Organizations and caregivers responding to short- or long-term disaster should include elements in their emergency or reconstruction programming that provide opportunities for releasing the energy from the body.

Trauma and the Brain

The human brain is designed to orchestrate the "fight or flight" and "freeze" responses in order to protect us, keeping us safe and alive. A part of the brain known as the emotional brain (limbic system) registers fear and sends a message to another part of the brain—the instinctual brain (brain stem)—that floods our body with stress hormones and chemicals for action. This happens automatically and very quickly and the thinking brain (cerebral cortex) is basically bypassed. This phenomenon severely compromises decision-making related to complex long-term planning and response. Individuals and communities can become immobilized. Disaster response needs to include body/mind/energy exercises to reintegrate the various parts of the brain for creative and clear thinking. Community members affected by disasters will need to experience a similar type of reintegration, often led by the efforts of local or external leaders. This involves being transparent regarding the issues at hand and possibilities for the future. Rumors must be stemmed, fears calmed, and real security increased through collective action or mutual care.

Trauma and Behavior

In STAR we say "hurt people hurt people." If the energy accumulated during the freeze response is not used in a productive way, it is often turned against ourselves or others. When we turn trauma energy against ourselves, we call it "acting-in" behavior, which includes addictions, eating disorders, depression, withdrawal, anxiety, self-blame, etc. When the trauma energy is turned against others, it is called "acting-out" behavior and may include criminal activity, repetitive conflicts, abuse, aggression, blaming, etc. It is not uncommon for persons who have experienced trauma to have difficulty relating to others. Cooperation and collective action can become more difficult. Hence, efforts to mobilize individuals and groups may be relatively unsuccessful if programs have not incorporated activities or processes in their response efforts to address trauma, such as the creation of a space for people to share stories or processes that help them engage with others they may perceive to be benefiting from greater levels of assistance or support.[7]

Trauma and Beliefs

Disasters often shatter our beliefs and sense of order in the world. Individuals wonder why God allowed the disaster to happen or if God still cares. Faith is often put to the test and sometimes strengthened. Moral standards may disappear or weaken. On the other hand, some persons may become even more rigid and unforgiving in their beliefs to the point of intolerance. The belief in an ordered world that allows us to go about our daily activity in a predictable fashion may be destroyed. Humans are meaning-making creatures and need to assign meaning to what happened. This is done by constructing narratives about what happened; these narratives can either move us forward or keep us stuck. Group rituals, compassionate listening, and support by extended family, church, or community can play an important role in helping people recover faith in their families, neighbors, and community and make meaning out of what they have experienced. Social scientists have discovered that communities with strong social ties tend to be able to heal quicker and rebuild more effectively.[8]

Trauma-sensitive humanitarian aid, reconstruction, and, eventually, development can all contribute to creating an environment that promotes resilience and well-being by providing some of the basic needs in a post-disaster situation and, at the same time, implementing programs that provide opportunities for individuals and communities to address the trauma and extreme stress. Since many organizations specialize in providing particular services, cooperation and collaboration among a wide range of organizations or community efforts is essential to make certain that a multi-disciplinary response addresses the multiply-wounded nature of a society in a post-disaster setting.[9]

QUESTIONS

1. What is resilience? How do we foster greater resiliency?
2. What does it mean to be "trauma-informed"?
3. What happens to our bodies when we experience trauma?
4. What do you think it means that "hurt people hurt people"?

THE CONGREGATIONAL TOOLKIT
Community Resources

18

Building Networks and Utilizing Community Resources

LURA CAYTON

Several months into the long-term recovery following Hurricanes Isidore and Lili in 2002, a group of pastors were meeting in one of the hardest hit communities, having a conversation about the experience of the previous months. One pastor, Jim, talked about how he and his family had evacuated out of the state. Once the storms passed, Jim was anxious to get back to the community to gather together the congregation he was serving. Jim described how stunned he was as he drove back home. Power lines were still down. Huge trees were laying, knocked over like toothpicks. The roofs were blown off of many homes, and there was extensive damage to most. Jim remembered saying to his wife, "I wonder how my church is going to help?" He wondered how the judicatory level of his denomination would help the congregation and the community. But, even more, he wondered how his congregation could respond. At that point he had no idea how members of the congregation had come through the disaster. He knew there would be much work for the congregation to do to get its building back in shape and to minister to the members and others in the community. However, he had no idea where to begin.

Jim is not alone. Most of us don't want to believe that disaster will happen in our community. However, the best way to be able to answer Jim's question is to begin preparing when there is no disaster. No single

Lura Cayton is an ordained minister in the Christian Church (Disciples of Christ). She has served Church World Service as a disaster response and recovery liaison with responsibility for community organizing for long-term recovery following domestic disaster, and as an emergency response specialist, providing training in long-term recovery and other areas of the disaster cycle. She currently works with FEMA as a reservist volunteer agency liaison specialist.

104

group can do by themselves everything that needs to be done to help a community recover; therefore, building relationships with others in your community is a good starting point. This assumes that you have encouraged members of the congregation to be personally prepared with a disaster plan and a survival kit, and have followed that advice yourself. It also assumes that the congregation has developed a disaster plan; has had the church building professionally inspected to determine the vulnerabilities to disaster; and has worked to mitigate those possibilities.

Looking around your community for potential collaborators in the face of a disaster helps a congregation begin to understand how the community is most susceptible and how to build resiliency[1] within the community. From there, efforts can be made to educate people with regard to ways to alleviate the dangers. When a disaster does happen, the response includes rescue, relief, and recovery. If connections have not been made before the disaster, it is a struggle to get organized in the midst of chaos, and to begin helping victims become survivors.

In the immediate aftermath of a disaster, many individuals and congregations want to help and will rush to take action. However, without preplanning, their efforts can be ineffective and even detrimental to the response and recovery efforts. Advance planning means the response can happen more rapidly and in a more organized manner. Resources will have been identified to help that process and can be used efficiently and effectively, and this is good stewardship.

Once the immediate needs of victim/survivors are addressed—people have food, water, clothes, basic medical attention if needed, and at least a temporary place to live—there will be others who need more extensive help. It will take the efforts and resources of the community, and possibly beyond, to help those hardest hit to arrive at a "new normal." Communities of all shapes and sizes must grapple with what sort of recovery the community will strive for following the disaster. Should only those with extensive resources recover well? Do you want even those who have limited personal resources to recover? To a large extent, the nature of the community following a disaster is determined by the preparations made prior to the disaster, including building community and identifying resources.

One of the other things you will want to do is to define your community geographically. Is it your neighborhood, city or town, county, or something else? You may want to begin to form some relationships and then determine your definition of geographic community. As you are forming the relationships and defining the community, you will also want to begin to catalogue resources. As you build relationships, work together to develop resources, create a plan, and develop a network that will be poised to respond to your community's needs. The following section will help guide the research you do, the strategies you construct, and the protocols you develop. Utilize the following questions as a means to construct your plans for responding and rebuilding.

A. What kind of relationships are needed?

1. *Relationships with other congregations from across the ecumenical spectrum.* No one group can do alone all that needs to be done.
   - Who are the other congregations in your community? How would you contact their leadership, before and after a disaster?
   - Is there a ministerial alliance or some other gathering of clergy? Is there more than one clergy group based on ethnic composition or theological position?
   - Is there a "council of churches" or other entity that gathers congregations together?

2. *Relationships with other faith/religious traditions.* Disaster is no respecter of particular faith groups.
   - What other faith traditions are in your community—Jewish, Muslim, Sikh, Hindu, Buddhist, or others?
   - Do you know how to contact them?
   - Consider how you can gather these groups. Such gatherings are not necessarily easy. Can you and others put aside your theological differences and other biases to prepare to help if your community or a neighboring community experiences a disaster? How can you learn more about each other so that each group will understand the others and what they might be doing in the immediate aftermath of a disaster and be able to contribute to developing a plan to coordinate the response?

3. *Relationships with your local emergency management agency and emergency manager and other governmental officials, including the Federal Emergency Management Agency (FEMA).* Government entities are going to be among the first responders and will manage and control access to the disaster site.
   - Who is your emergency manager? Check with your state VOAD, local city, county, or state government offices.
   - What is the disaster plan for your community? Check with your local government officials and state VOAD.
   - Is the religious community included in the disaster plan?
   - Do the community first responders "exercise" any disaster plan or run any sort of drills? Is the faith community included in the "exercise"?
   - Who is the FEMA Voluntary Agency Liaison (VAL) for your FEMA

region—and what region are you in? How can the VAL help you build relationships?

- What other government agencies participate in disaster response and recovery?

4. *Relationships with the agencies that provide social services to your community.* Many social service agencies will find their case loads increased and may also have special disaster programs.

- What are the social service agencies in your community? This would include your Department of Social Services, but would also include programs for seniors, children, and families; food banks; faith-based groups that provide food, clothes, etc.

5. *Relationships with other disaster response organizations.* There are a number of organizations that have extensive experience in all phases of disaster. Your Church World Service Emergency Response Specialist[2] can help you identify those organizations.

- What organizations are members or partners of the National Voluntary Organizations Active in Disaster (VOAD)? What resources do these organizations provide in each phase of disaster? How do you contact them and under what circumstances do they provide their resources?
- What organizations are members or partners of your state VOAD?
- Is there a local VOAD or a Community Organizations Active in Disaster (COAD)? Do you need to start one?
- Is your religious tradition a part of VOAD?
- Have you talked with the American Red Cross about what it means to open your building as a shelter or feeding site if there is a disaster?
- Have you participated in American Red Cross training for sheltering and mass care following a disaster?
- What other trainings are offered that would better prepare you to help your community? How do you identify community resources that can be a part of the recovery process when your community experiences a disaster?

B. What is your community and what are the resources in your community?

1. *What boundaries make sense?*

- Are you a part of a large metropolitan area where the city makes sense as your community?
- Are you in a very rural area where your community is multi-county?
- Is your county a community?
- What are the service areas for the social services? And what

geographic areas are covered by the religious groups?

2. *What assets are there in your community?*
   - Map the assets of your community. Asset Mapping is a positive approach to a community developed by John Kretzmann and John McKnight. By mapping your community you identify what is already available in the community, and by building relationships with and among the "assets" you will be better prepared to respond to a disaster.
   - What are the gifts, skills, and capabilities of individuals within your community? It helps to identify community leadership who may lead the way in the case of a disaster.
   - What are the informal networks and groups within the community that help to accomplish various purposes and activities within the community? It helps to identify neighborhood organizations, clubs, and social groups that can be allies and the source of resources for preparedness, response, and recovery.
   - What are the formal structures and institutions within the community? It helps to identify businesses, schools, social services, cultural resources, health care resources, and economic development resources for all phases of disaster.

C. What are the physical and social vulnerabilities in your community that are exacerbated by a disaster?

1. *What are the physical vulnerabilities in your community that could lead to a disaster:*
   - Common weather threats?
   - Other potential natural disaster hazards?
   - Locations of potential toxic spills?
   - Transportation methods and corridors that carry hazardous materials through the community—trains, trucks, etc.?

2. *What social factors cause some people within the community to be more vulnerable to disasters:*
   - Lack of affordable housing?
   - Limited access to resources?
   - Limited access to political structures?
   - Language barriers?
   - Limited education?
   - Limited employment?
   - Limited income?
   - Limited access to transportation?
   - Lack of social support?
   - Lack of preparedness for disaster?

• Who are these people and where do they live in the community?

D. What resources are made available by a Presidential Disaster Declaration?

- What is the process for securing a disaster declaration?
- If there is a Presidentially Declared Disaster that includes Individual Assistance, what is the sequence of delivery of federal resources to individuals and households?
- What other Federal Resources may be available?
- What resources will be available if there is not a disaster declaration?
- Does your state make provision for a State Individual Assistance Disaster Declaration? What resources does it make available?

Though extensive, this list of questions is not exhaustive... And, I promise, after finding some answers you and your community will never be the same.

HELPFUL WEBSITES

National VOAD: www.nvoad.org
Extension Disaster Education Network: www.eden.lsu.edu
CWS Emergency Response Program: www.cwserp.org
CWS Community Arise Curriculum: www.communityarise.com
CWS Resource "Managing & Operating a Disaster Long-Term Recovery Organization," available at: www.disasterrecoveryhelp.info
FEMA: www.fema.gov
Resources following Presidential Declarations of Disaster: www.disasterassistance.gov
The Red Cross: www.redcross.org
A Resource from the United Church of Christ for Technologically Based Disasters: http://www.ucc.org/disaster/technology-disasters/Silent-Disaster-Draft-Final-4-7-08.pdf

BOOKS

Brenda D. Phillips et al., eds., *Social Vulnerability to Disaster* (Boca Raton: CRC Press, 2010).
John Kretzmann and John McKnight, *Building Communities from the Inside Out: A Path Toward Finding and Mobilizing a Community's Assets* (1993).

19

Systems and Supplies

Some Lists and Tasks for Preparing Your Congregation for a Disaster

BARRY SHADE AND BRIAN CROUSURE

Checklist for Congregational Disaster Preparedness

Local churches as well as individuals are vulnerable to hazards. In addition to establishing networks and putting communication systems in place, the governing body of a local church may find the following checklist helpful in planning for disaster preparedness.

The most obvious and first area to explore will be the building, grounds, and resources belonging to or used by the local church.

If the building is up to code, explore additional safety measures:

- Install sprinklers and/or centralized fire alarms throughout the building
- Connect fire alarm to fire department dispatch center
- Make sure smoke detectors work and are powered by fresh batteries
- As a church, appoint a "fire marshal"/safety coordinator who reports directly to the governing body at least every six months

Brian Crousure, a United Church of Christ minister, has been involved in disaster response and recovery most of his life. He has responded to tornadoes, floods, hurricanes, and mass casualty incidents as a survivor, pastor, hospital chaplain, and Church World Service disaster response specialist.

Barry Shade serves as associate director for domestic emergency response for CWS. He has served as a FEMA disaster assistance employee who has been deployed to Louisiana, Iowa, Alabama, Kansas, and Nebraska. He also served in the United States Air Force, providing expertise in disaster preparedness.

Conduct an interior safety inspection at least every six months to identify and eliminate hazards such as these:

- Materials stored in evacuation stairs and hallways
- Materials stored in furnace rooms/other sources of ignition
- Not enough fully charged and inspected fire extinguishers of appropriate types at every exit, in kitchen, in sanctuary and nursery, in office area, and other places where necessary
- Nonworking emergency lighting system (egress lighting, exit signs)
- No flashlights with working batteries next to fire extinguishers
- Fire doors opened when they should remain closed
- Trip and fall hazards
- Other hazards to life, safety, and health

Conduct an exterior safety inspection at least every six months to identify and eliminate hazards:

- Shrubs, bushes, and other obstructions hiding or blocking doors and windows
- Combustible materials too near the building
- Deadwood, brush, firewood on the premises
- Inadequate lighting of parking areas and entrance areas
- Missing exterior signage directing fire department to occupied areas
- No security fencing appropriate to the neighborhood
- Broken, uneven, or missing sidewalks and curb-cuts
- No designated handicapped parking, handicapped-accessible entrances and exits, as well as ramps
- Broken windows, window locks, or other means of unauthorized entry
- Keys hidden in-easy-to find locations such as an outdoor key box or "Knox Box"
- Broken, obstructed, or missing gutters, downspouts, or drains to take water at least fifteen feet from foundation
- Obstructed sump pump/air conditioner/furnace discharge or flues
- Other unique hazards

If the building is not up to Life Safety Code and/or the Americans with Disabilities Act, even if not required to do so by local authorities, take the following actions:

- Contact local authorities for inspections and recommendations
- Budget monies above regular maintenance for improvement
- Make a plan

~ Appoint a safety officer with responsibility to identify hazards and recommend remediation to the governing body
~ Begin to conduct safety inspections (see above) every six months
~ Identify and triage the hazards
~ Prioritize the work to be done and identify who will do it
~ Address the most glaring needs first
~ Re-evaluate the plan regularly

Even more important than protecting the building is safeguarding the life, safety, and health of the persons participating in the local church's life.

• Does the church have a policy ensuring physical, emotional, psychological, and sexual safety of all participants in the church's life?
  ~ If yes, good for you. Review it and make sure that appropriate procedures and personnel are identified to ensure its implementation and enforcement.
  ~ If not, contact your denomination, association, or other connectional body, or the church's insurance carrier for recommendations and assistance.
• Recruit a church CERT (Citizens Emergency Response Team). This is a group of trained volunteers (free training available through city/county Emergency Management) who are equipped to assist others before professional fire, medical, or other authorities can reach disaster-affected persons.
• Is there appropriate signage inside and outside the building directing persons to severe weather safe areas? (It doesn't work to say: "In the event of a tornado, go to the choir room" if the Boy Scouts, AA members, neighborhood children, or others using the building have no idea where the choir room is.)
• Is the local church prepared to "shelter in place," that is, shelter its members within the church building should an emergency happen during worship or other church event? (Possible hazards: an unexpected blizzard, ice storm, a chemical spill, or other event causing the local church to shelter in place the number of people typically in the building for a worship service.)
• Is there space, food, water, toileting supplies, and blankets sufficient to sustain the usual number of attendees at morning worship in the building for up to 72 hours?
• Conduct a "shelter in place" drill as a part of Disaster Preparedness Month or National Tornado Awareness Day.
• Is the local church prepared to evacuate quickly and safely?

~ Are there clearly marked evacuation routes?

~ Is there a clearly identified outside gathering place where a roll can be taken to assure that everyone is out of the building safely?

- Are there persons identified and prepared to assist mobility-limited, sight-impaired, or other types of persons needing assistance to evacuate?

- Are Sunday school teachers and nursery attendants prepared to evacuate their charges, and are parents willing to trust that others will evacuate their children rather than impeding evacuation by rushing to their children?

Does the local church have a Continuity of Operations Plan (COOP) that covers:

- Relocation from destroyed or damaged facilities to a preidentified alternate location for worship, staff working space, fellowship space, etc.

- Off-site daily back-up of financial records

- Off-site back-up of mailing, phone, and e-mail lists

- Off-site back-up of historical and membership records

- Continuation of essential ministries

- Redundant means of communications with participants concerning emergencies and contingencies.

Leadership is critical! One of the unfortunate but preventable effects of disasters is the loss of lay, pastoral, religious, or other leadership. Safeguarding the leadership is also critical. In preparing for disasters, the governing body of a local church may wish to consider some of the following ideas to prevent job stress, compassion fatigue, burn-out, and displaced anger. While the pastoral staff may be the most obvious persons to be affected, the church secretary, the lay leaders of mission or volunteer groups, or others who regularly come into contact with disaster survivors may experience any one of those effects.

- Does the governing body understand that a disaster affecting the church and/or the community will require the attention of the pastoral leadership?

- The governing body may consider an addition to the pastor's (or other staff) job description clearly stating that participation in response and recovery efforts will become a priority and will take precedence over other "normal" activities. Will the lay leadership take a proactive role in communicating this to the membership and in addressing persons who displace anger about the disaster onto the pastor (an all too frequent occurrence)?

- Does the connectional relationship provide for "back-up" for a pastor in a disaster affected community, allowing the pastor to concentrate on response and recovery while others share the load of visiting, worship preparation, administration, and other duties?
- Will the local church provide for a paid leave for the pastoral staff (anywhere from a weekend retreat to months-long sabbatical, depending on the situation) following a disaster or during an extended disaster response?
- Will the local church arrange for a caregiver for the caregivers (counselor or chaplain) during and after a disaster, and pay for that service if necessary?

Hazards and Vulnerabilities

A disaster happens when a *hazard* affects a population that is *vulnerable* to that particular hazard. A tornado in a Kansas wheat field is not necessarily a disaster; the same tornado unexpectedly hitting a crowded neighborhood is.

An important step early in the process of disaster response preparation is to identify what hazards exist in the community and who is vulnerable to them. People need to make a distinction between what is "probable" versus what is "possible." While a terrorist attack or airliner crash in a neighborhood is "possible," it is not "probable." Tornadoes, floods, hazardous materials events, and other hazards are more probable. People should identify and prepare for the probable and not waste time and resources on the less likely events. Identification of hazards can happen in family, neighborhood, church, and community settings (see Fig. 19-1 on next page).

Fig. 19-1: **Hazards and Vulnerabilities Checklist**

A disaster happens when a hazard affects a population vulnerable to that particular hazard. A tornado in a Kansas wheat field is not a disaster while the same tornado unexpectedly hitting a crowded neighborhood is. The first step in individual or congregational preparedness is identifying what hazards exist in the community and who is vulnerable to them. Identify the hazards that are probable in your neighborhood. People need to make a distinction between what is "probable" versus what is "possible". While a terrorist attack or airliner crash in a neighborhood is "possible," it is not "probable". Tornadoes, floods, hazardous materials events, and other hazards are more probable. People should identify and prepare for the probable and not waste time and resources on the unlikely, possible events. Identification of hazards can happen in family, neighborhood, church, and community settings.

ALL HAZARDS

Everybody is vulnerable to some hazards—whether caused by natural events or human action, deliberate or inadvertent.

Preparedness Steps

1. Visit www.ready.gov for more information and suggestions
2. Make and write two plans:
   a. A shelter in place plan
   b. An evacuation plan.
   c. Practice each plan at least once a year with every member of the household.
3. Have a disaster kit for sheltering in place stored in the safest room in your home or in the pre-identified place to which you will retreat when a hazard is threatening. With this kit, be prepared to be self-sufficient for 72 hours for food, water, essential medicines, toileting facilities, protection from dangerous weather, receiving emergency information (NOAA radio with extra batteries, essential communications (2 way radio, disposable cell phone, walkietalkie, all with extra batteries). Have a low-tech means of signaling for help (horn, whistle, flashlight)
4. Have a second kit for evacuation and keep it near the door. With this kit, be prepared to go to a preidentified retreat (a friend or relative's home, a public disaster shelter, or a spontaneous shelter site). This kit should, at a minimum, include three days' supply of:
   a. essential medicines,
   b. a sheet of essential contact and medical information for each family member,
   c. shelf-stable food (energy bars, etc), bottled water,
   d. comfort toys for small children,
   e. blankets, toilet paper.
5. Prepare a flash drive of essential information (see appendix)

TORNADO

Every state in the US has experienced a tornado so all persons should be prepared. But, some persons are more vulnerable than others.
- People who live in areas where tornadoes are common occurrences.
- People who live in mobile homes or homes without basements.
- People with physical or other limitations to seeking shelter quickly.
- People who live in areas without warning sirens or other means of emergency alert communications.

Preparedness Steps
1. Shelter in place plan and kits (see above).
2. NOAA weather radio(s) located where the alerts can be heard through-out the dwelling.
3. Pre-identified, always accessible, shelter (if no in-home safe room).

FLOODING FROM A NUMBER OF SOURCES

- River and stream overtopping banks/levees
- Overland flooding from excessive rain/snowmelt.
- Hurricane and/or storm surge
- Dam and/or dike failures
- Sewer back-up
- Hydrostatic pressure forcing water into basements or low-lying structures.

Preparedness Steps
1. Shelter in place plan and evacuation plans and kits (see above).
2. NOAA weather radio(s) located where the alerts can be heard through-out the dwelling.
3. Buy flood insurance from the National Flood Insurance Program (NFIP). HOMEOWNERS, RENTERS, AND MORTGAGE INSURANCE DOES NOT COVER FLOODING. Go to www.floodsafe.gov for details and to locate an agent.
4. Mitigate against damage in basements by elevating furnace, hot water heater, appliances.
5. Purchase a high capacity utility or sump pump with discharge to the outside

HURRICANE

- Winds, tornadoes, blowing debris
- Flooding, storm surge
- Loss of utilities and services

At Risk
- Anybody living along the Atlantic or Gulf Coast.
- The elderly, people with mobility difficulties, the disabled, the homeless
- People in homes not built to hurricane resistant standards
- People without transportation out of harm's way
- People without access to timely emergency information

Preparedness Steps
1. Shelter in place plan and evacuation plans and kits (see above).
2. NOAA weather radio(s) located where the alerts can be heard through-out the dwelling.
3. Establish a reliable means for assuring that vulnerable family members, neighbors, church members have the means to evacuate to a safe, sanitary, secure, and functional retreat
4. Agree ahead of time that everyone will evacuate when local government officials recommend it or order it.
5. Identify and agree on what you will take in addition to persons and pets
6. Identify the evacuation route (and an alternate) that you will use and practice before a hurricane is imminent
7. When a hurricane is forecast, secure a full tank of gas and keep it full
8. If sheltering in place, identify the area of the home for sheltering that is least susceptible to wind damage and flooding
9. Assist community organizations who help the homeless during emergencies

EXTREME WEATHER EVENTS
   • Blizzards, extreme cold, unusual accumulation of snow/ice
   • Excessive heat, high humidity, drought,
   • Straight line winds, dust storms, etc.

At Risk
   • The elderly, people with breathing difficulties, other medical conditions, the disabled, small children.
   • People in homes with either too little or too much exposure to outside air/temperature
   • Homeless persons

Preparedness Steps
1. Shelter plan in place and evacuation plans and kits (see above).
2. NOAA weather radio(s) located where the alerts can be heard through-out the dwelling.
3. Establish a reliable means for checking on vulnerable family members, neighbors, church members.
4. Identify the area of the home for sheltering that is least susceptible to heat loss or gain
5. Maintain a supply of blankets, sleeping bags, winter clothing
6. Have a push-broom with very long handle for removing snow from porches, carports, etc. with having to climb on a ladder
7. Have a non-electric means of heating food and water (woodstove, fireplace, Sterno stove, etc. NEVER USE CHARCOAL/GAS GRILLS INSIDE unless safely placed on non-combustible surface and properly vented through a chimney)
8. When high heat warnings are issued, freeze extra containers of water to use if electricity is interrupted.
9. Assist community organizations who host the homeless during emergencies

The Survival Flash Drive:
Disaster Preparedness for Information Safety

We live in an information age. Our personal/family/church information tends to be kept in a variety of places and may not be easily safeguarded in the event of a disaster. Protect yourself by scanning all your important documents (see Fig. 19-2 on next page for examples) for each member of the family (including children away at college, in the military, or other remote locations) and storing them on a *Survival Flash Drive* (also known as thumb drive, memory stick, etc.). Create an easy-to-remember password to limit access. Make several copies and label each with the family name and the designation "I.C.E." ("in case of emergency").

Put them in the following locations:

- Your shelter in place and evacuation kits
- Your bank safe deposit box
- At your work place(s) in a secure desk or locker
- With a trusted family member or friend not likely to be affected by the same disaster.

Fig. 19-2: **The Survival Flash Drive**

Disaster Preparedness For Information Safety

We live in an information age. Our personal/family/church information tends to be kept in a variety of places and may not be easily safeguarded in the event of a disaster. Protect yourself by scanning all your important documents for each member of the family (including children away at college, in the military, or other remote locations) and storing them on a Survival Flash Drive (also known as thumb drive, memory stick, etc). Create an easy to remember password to limit access. Make several copies and label each with the family name and the designation ICE (in case of emergency). Put them in the following locations:

- Your shelter in place and evacuation kits
- Your bank safe deposit box
- At your work place(s) in a secure desk or locker
- With a trusted family member or friend not likely to be affected by the same disaster

Personal Information

- Current photos of each member of the family, including children away at college or other reasons
- Important family and pet pictures
- Emergency contact list for immediate and extended family and friends
- Wills and Advanced Directives

Health Records

- Copies of Health Plan cards, prescription, eye, and other health insurance
- Medical Records, history, diagnoses
- Copies of prescriptions
- Vaccination Records
- Powers of Attorney for health care decisions

Official Government Documents

- Driver's Licenses or state IDs/Passport/Visas for each family member
- Permits, and Certifications
- Veteran/Discharge Papers
- Birth/Adoption Certificate
- Marriage Certificate
- Work Permits / Licenses
- Social Security Card
- Immigration Papers
- Court documents relating to divorce, custody, alimony, child support criminal proceedings, Restraining orders

Financial Records

- Bank Accounts, including checking acct routing number, savings account information, CD's, and Credit Card Accounts;
- Real Estate / Mortgage documents,
- Insurance Policies (life, health, homeowners, flood, car, personal property, burial/cremation
- Business Records
- Rental Agreements
- Tax records (Form 1040 pages 1 and 2 for the past 3 years
- Contracts
- Warranties on major appliances and equipment

Other unique documents that you may need

- Will differ based on individual/family

What Can Denominational Agencies and Parachurch Organizations Offer?

A Case Study

CHRISTY SMITH

This essay describes ways the United Methodist Committee on Relief (UMCOR) can be a resource following a disaster. Many denominations and religious associations have similar resources. Several are listed at the end of this essay. Check with your local church leadership, middle judicatory, or national office to learn more about what services your church might access.

Vision

As the humanitarian relief and development arm of The United Methodist Church, UMCOR transforms and strengthens people and communities.

Mission

Compelled by Christ to be a voice of conscience on behalf of the people called Methodist, UMCOR works globally to alleviate human suffering and advance hope and healing.

Even before the water overflows, the wind blows, and the earth quivers, the people of God seek ways to follow the mandate to be a very present neighbor to those who are devastated in the myriad ways

Christy Smith is a staff member of the United Methodist Committee on Relief (UMCOR).

AT A GLANCE

UMCOR helps:

Prepare for disasters. UMCOR works cooperatively with annual conferences in the event of an emergency and to prepare for emergencies. We work through the disaster response coordinator to provide training in all aspects of disaster response.

Respond to disasters. UMCOR always responds to emergencies at the invitation of and through the affected annual conference. In addition to providing training, UMCOR offers technical assistance and support through a highly trained network of staff, consultants, and experienced volunteers to help annual conferences respond to all phases of a disaster.

Recover from disasters. UMCOR can send emergency grants immediately to fund start-up relief activities. UMCOR also supports long-term recovery ministries through the provision of grants, planning, technical assistance, and training, and helps coordinate volunteers. All requests for assistance are received through the conference disaster coordinator.

disasters overwhelm communities. For congregations, that ministry effort often begins with the anticipation of those catastrophes that *might* strike damaging blows. But, for too many faith communities, disaster response happens, all too literally, *on the fly*.

The United Methodist Church, through its humanitarian and relief agency, United Methodist Committee on Relief (UMCOR), has been at work since 1941 to respond to natural and human-caused crises. What UMCOR believes is that responding in the name of God involves passion, commitment, and training; all directed by spiritual wisdom and discernment. When guided by the compassion that is at the heart of the Christian faith, United Methodists join their faith partners in ministry that is centered on the teachings of Jesus Christ. Therefore, we follow United Methodist progenitor John Wesley's advice to do no harm, do good, and stay in love with God.

Best practices for responding in these ways are incorporated into all UMCOR trainings. The training menu, available at www.UMCOR. org, provides current material that not only can adapt to changes in United Methodist polity and procedures, but also to emerging needs in the disaster response arena.

As of 2012, those trainings generally included basic information about disaster response, courses on spiritual and emotional care basics, classes to prepare disaster case managers, local church preparation, volunteer preparation and coordination, and early response team training, as well as classes on disasters and creation care.[1]

It helps to understand how UMCOR's U.S. Disaster Program provides support to congregations. UMCOR offers its resources, both training and material, through its conferences.[2] Therefore, most local church programs are accessed through each conference's designee, its disaster response coordinator.

Because United Methodist disaster response coordinators also participate in state and faith-based disaster response connections, requests for UMCOR's presence might come from another partner faith group or agency. UMCOR does not limit its trainings to United Methodists, though conferences may request particular trainings for particular United Methodist groups or churches. The conference disaster response coordinator makes the decision about fielding a request to UMCOR's Disaster Relief office in Washington, D.C.

One of the training opportunities UMCOR offers is *Connecting Neighbors*, a course that can provide intensive training for those who wish to lead conferences, districts, and congregations in preparing for disaster. It is also geared for use at the local church level. Uniquely United Methodist in the portions relating to United Methodist policies and procedures, it is also broadly accessible and relevant for any congregation seeking to be prepared for and respond to disaster.

The premise of *Connecting Neighbors* is that we are only able to respond to others out of strength. The traveler in Jesus' parable, wounded and bleeding, could not have helped anyone. The Good Samaritan—prepared with heart, mind, and resources—was able to assist. Just the same, churches need to "expect the unexpected" and develop disaster plans to assure that each member of the church and the neighboring community is "ready," that their church is physically and fiscally prepared to sustain a response, and that they have identified areas of ministry that are unique to the church's resources—physical, professional, spiritual, and material. Only then can they respond out of strength.

The course focuses churches on mitigating the hazards around the church's property, considering insurance issues and liability for ministries that might emerge from disaster, protecting church records, and making sure the members and the church are as prepared as possible to enter into ministry following disaster.

There are churches along the Gulf Coast that washed away when Hurricane Katrina hit; for the ones that had not protected precious photographs, birth and death records, marriages and membership rolls by keeping copies off-site, the physical records of the history of that congregation is gone forever. Preparation could have lessened the loss that the already-impacted community sustained.

Do churches go to work to respond even though they've never considered disaster ministry? Certainly. And most do a remarkable job. There were also churches after Katrina that responded to meet the needs of others, even though they had holes in their own roofs. The people of God will find a way. UMCOR suggests that pre-planning, training, and education will dramatically multiply a church's ability to respond.

Disaster ministry gives churches a unique opportunity to be the visible presence of God to those suffering a wide range of calamities. Who can bind the hurting heart better? Within every congregation are those who do not believe they have anything to offer following a disaster. "I can't climb a ladder or drive a nail," they might say, "so there is nothing for me to do."

However, there is a ministry for every person within a church and every church. UMCOR helps connect those gifts with tasks needed following a disaster. Consider the tiny church in North Carolina that consisted of a handful of seniors every Sunday morning. Their only resource was a group of women who could cook, so following a hurricane, they began cooking…and cooking…and cooking. Others joined in. Soon, not only survivors but disaster responders and the impacted community were gathering for meals—a ministry of hospitality given life from a tiny spark of willingness and few visible resources.

Another church, after watching television coverage about the horrifying impact on the pets lost in Katrina, formed a disaster response ministry uniquely aimed at helping disaster survivors evacuate along with their pets.

It isn't uncommon for survivors to greet responders with the words: "I knew God would send someone." Denominational and parachurch organizations such as UMCOR help prepare, train, and empower people to be the "someones" who reach out when disasters strike.

Denominational, Parachurch, and Ecumenical Organizations Involved in Disaster Response

■ **Church World Service** — www.churchworldservice.org

CWS's Emergency Response Program focuses on both immediate emergency assistance and long-term support that helps survivors take ownership of the recovery process.

■ **One Great Hour of Sharing** — onegreathourofsharing.org

An offering that makes the love of Christ real for individuals and communities around the world who suffer the effects of disaster, conflict, or severe economic hardship, and for those who serve them through gifts of money and time. Today, projects are underway in more than 100 countries, including the United States and Canada. While specific allocations differ in each of the nine participating denominations, all use their One Great Hour of Sharing funds to make possible disaster relief, refugee assistance, development aid, and more.

■ **Week of Compassion—www.weekofcompassion.org**

The Relief, Refugee, and Development Fund of the Christian Church (Disciples of Christ)

■ **Disciples Volunteering—www.discipleshomemissions.org/dhm/ dhm- ministries/volunteering/volunteering-disaster-response/**

The ministry of Disciples Volunteering is focused on "serving in mission": calling, connecting, equipping and blessing Disciples for service. Disciples Volunteering is equipped to resource congregations when a disaster strikes their community. When people "Get Dirty for Jesus" they experience life-changing, congregational-transforming revitalization.

■ **United Methodist Committee on Relief—www.umcor.org**

UMCOR offers disaster preparedness training, provides essential supplies and care—both physical and psychological—in the immediate aftermath of a disaster, and supports long-term rebuilding efforts and assists communities as they adapt.

■ **Presbyterian Church-U.S.A-Presbyterian Disaster Assistance (PDA)— www.presbyterianmission.org/ministries/pda/**

PDA is an emergency and refugee program focusing on the long-term recovery of disaster impacted communities. Volunteer work teams help families rebuild and restore their homes, or to do other disaster recovery work.

■ **United Church of Christ—www.ucc.org**

The UCC Office of National Disaster Ministries provides assistance with acute and/or long-term effects of natural or technologically-caused disasters.

■ **Brethren Disaster Ministries—www.brethren.org/bdm/**

Brethren Disaster Ministries restores hope for the most vulnerable disaster survivors by engaging volunteers to repair and rebuild storm-damaged homes, and by providing grants to support the disaster recovery efforts of faith-based partners.

■ **Nazarene Disaster Response—ncmusacan.nazarene.org/NDR/ tabid/665/Default.html**

Nazarene Disaster Response is Nazarenes mobilizing for disasters through readiness, response, and recovery.

■ **Mennonite Disaster Services—mds.mennonite.net/**

Mennonite Disaster Service is a volunteer network of Anabaptist churches that responds to those affected by disaster in Canada and the United States.

■ **International Disaster and Emergency Services — ides.org/**

IDES' vision is to lead the independent Christian Churches/Churches of Christ in responding to disasters and emergencies in the United States and throughout the world by mobilizing financial and physical resources to and through their missionaries and congregations.

■ **Episcopal Relief and Development — www.er-d.org/**

ERD is an international relief and development agency serving on behalf of the Episcopal Church of the United States.

■ **The Southern Baptist Convention/North American Mission Board — www.namb.net/dr/**

The Mission Board serves through the local church to bring help, healing, and hope to individuals and communities affected by disaster.

■ **Churches of Christ Disaster Relief Effort — disasterreliefeffort.org/**

The Churches of Christ Disaster Relief Effort immediately responds to any major disaster in the continental United States by sending truckloads of emergency food, water, cleaning, and other supplies to disaster victims through a local Church of Christ working with us in the area of the disaster.

■ **Churches of Christ Disaster Response Team — www.churchesofchristdrt.org**

The purpose of the Disaster Response Team is to aid the local congregation in recruiting and receiving volunteers to assist with the emotional and spiritual needs of the disaster victims and to assist them in the clean-up and rebuilding stage.

■ **Lutheran Disaster Response — www.ldr.org**

LDR promotes hope, healing, and wholeness for disaster survivors by providing spiritual and emotional care, long-term recovery resources, and volunteer coordination.

■ **World Renew — www.worldrenew.net**

World Renew volunteers give their time and talent to help clear debris, assess needs, and rebuild homes after a disaster strikes. CRWRC partners with NVOAD and Church World Services.

■ **American Baptist Churches USA — www.abhms.org/disaster_response/index.cfm**

The American Baptist Church's office of Direct Human Services provides financial assistance in every region of the United States in the name of American Baptist Churches USA.

This financial assistance meets immediate needs of disaster victims — for food, shelter, clothing, and medical care.

■ **Salvation Army—www.salvationarmyusa.org/**

The Salvation Army's disaster program consists of several basic services: food service, shelter, emergency financial assistance to individuals and families through casework specialists, donation management, emotional and spiritual care, emergency communications, disaster case management, clean-up and reconstruction, and partnerships.

■ **Adventist Development Relief Agency—www.adra.org**

ADRA seeks to identify and address social injustice and deprivation in developing countries. The agency's work seeks to improve the quality of life of those in need. ADRA invests in the potential of these individuals through community development initiatives targeting food security, economic development, primary health, and basic education. ADRA's emergency management initiatives provide aid to disaster survivors.

■ **The ACT Alliance—www.actalliance.org/**

ACT Alliance is a coalition of more than 140 churches and affiliated organizations working together in 140 countries to create positive and sustainable change in the lives of poor and marginalized people regardless of their religion, politics, gender, sexual orientation, race, or nationality in keeping with the highest international codes and standards. ACT mobilizes about $1.5 billion for its work each year in three targeted areas: humanitarian aid, development, and advocacy.

■ **National Volunteer Organizations Active in Disaster—www.nvoad.org/**

National Voluntary Organizations Active in Disaster (VOAD) is a nonprofit, nonpartisan, membership-based organization that serves as the forum where organizations share knowledge and resources throughout the disaster cycle—preparation, response, and recovery —to help disaster survivors and their communities.

For a complete list of members, which include faith-based and other organizations, visit http://www.nvoad.org/members.

Tips for Volunteer and Work Groups

Follow the Need, Not the News

In most communities affected by disasters, recovery takes several years. Developing the right structures to identify appropriate work and support volunteers takes time and coordination. The disaster-hit area you see on the news in July may not be ready for unskilled or skilled volunteers until the next March or April. Meanwhile, there may be a need for volunteers in a community affected by a past disaster that has dropped off of the media radar. If your church participates in a denominational, ecumenical, or parachurch disaster ministry, inquire about opportunities to serve before deciding on your group's destination.

Find a Good Partner

Your denomination may not have the right worksite match for your work group, depending on the distance you're able to travel or the level of skill your group has. Scheduling issues may mean you have to identify another partner. If you do, make sure the organization provides a safe environment for working, appropriate facilities for sleeping and cleaning up, and that the responsibilities of the partner and your work group are clear. Are you responsible for your own meals or are meals provided? Are all parties clear on liability in the event of an accident (and are there forms that must be signed)? Are materials provided by the partner or the work group? Having a partner you can trust ensures a better experience, especially for first-time volunteers.

Choose a partner organization that empowers the local community and encourages volunteers to work alongside and interact with a community's members. Learning the stories of the members of the community you serve is an important part of disaster recovery.

Build Enthusiasm, Build Community

Whether you are recruiting seasoned volunteers for a yearly work group, providing information to youth who are uncertain about their first volunteer work trip, or waking up after a fitful night's sleep on an air mattress on the first morning of your work trip, encourage your group to get to know one another, learn new skills, and be open to and excited about what their time of service will bring.

Organize some pre-trip meetings to help your group become familiar with one another, know what to expect, and get excited. Emphasize that a work trip is an opportunity to not only contribute one's skills but to build relationships with people in the community you are serving.

Make sure your group packs the appropriate clothing and equipment, and leaves unnecessary items at home. For some settings, technology (iPads and iPods, etc.) may not be appropriate and may discourage community building. Rely on your local recovery partner's advice, and set boundaries on their usage, as appropriate.

Emphasize that skills of all kinds can be used. Work trip groups need experienced workers; people who aren't experienced but are willing to learn; volunteers to run errands; cooks; folks who can organize and clean; and leaders who can motivate, coach, and recognize when people need to rest and take a break. When people feel empowered to use the skills they have, they will participate more fully—and are more likely to enjoy stepping outside their comfort zones to learn new skills.

Be Accurate in Reporting Your Skills

Most disaster recovery organizations like to know what they can expect from volunteers and will often send your group a form or questionnaire to survey the skill levels of your group members. Make sure these offer an accurate representation of your group's experience, skill, and ability. The local recovery organization, the volunteer groups that are scheduled in the weeks after your trip, and, most importantly, the members of the community you are serving are relying on the work of volunteers. If a volunteer group is assigned a task they can't do—or can only fake their way through—a person's property can be further damaged, unexpected expenses can accrue, and the recovery can be slowed down. Enthusiasm to learn new skills and try new things is important, but misrepresenting your skill level helps no one and could become dangerous.

Seek Age-Appropriate Work

Recovery organizations have good reasons for their age limits. Sometimes those limits exist because of state or local laws. Sometimes limits are established because of the number of work site supervisors available or the physical demands of a particular task. While you, as a group leader, may feel that you have an exceptionally mature or experienced youth who is younger than a stated age limit, or you may want to organize a family mission trip using a work partner that cannot accommodate youth or children, accept the guidance of your local partners. They know their context and capacity and have good reasons for the rules they have established.

Be Ready to Adapt

Disaster recovery is not an easy process for a community. Mistakes will happen. Not everything runs as efficiently as volunteers would like. Not everything makes sense to an outsider visiting for a week. Work groups sometimes arrive assuming they would be rebuilding houses for individual families, only to be assigned to build a playground at a public park. They were disappointed, as they believed their mission was to help people get back into their homes; when the local partner explained that helping create green space in an economically vulnerable neighborhood that was impacted by the tornado was part of the recovery plan, they jumped in with enthusiasm.

Though your volunteer group may bring a good amount of experience, it's important to respect the guidance of the local partner. The way you hope to serve may not be the way you are needed to serve.

Stewardship

Be responsible with the resources with which you have been entrusted.

For some groups, this may mean serving close to home to keep costs low enough that a wide variety of folks can travel. For others, it may mean sleeping on the floor of a host church en route rather than a more comfortable hotel. Some groups may choose to take a long caravan ride rather than flying across multiple states in order to reduce the group's carbon footprint. Talk about this with your leadership and/or as a group.

Provide Feedback in Appropriate Ways

Many recovery organizations will provide some sort of form or other mechanism for providing feedback. If you receive a survey at the end of a work trip, fill it out accurately, provide honest comments, and turn it in. Even the best recovery effort is a work in progress. Good, constructive criticism and recommendations about what works help make a recovery process even better for the next group.

If something went really wrong or seems inappropriate, however, make sure the right people know.

HAVE FUN!

Take some time—an afternoon or an evening—to explore the local culture of the community you're serving: a unique restaurant, a museum focused on local history, or a local state park or nature preserve can provide insight into the history and future of the community.

Be open to what you encounter on this unique adventure. Try new things. Above all, bring the joy that comes from putting your compassion into action with you! This is holy work.

Some Disaster Dos and Don'ts

These suggestions draw upon the experience and knowledge of Faith-Based Disaster Response Organizations, colleagues from FEMA, and the amazing volunteers who make up community-based Long-Term Recovery Committees.

Even if your community has not experienced a disaster, these suggestions are great to keep on hand in the event of a disaster affecting your community. They make a good resource to copy and hand out, post or project in your fellowship hall, or share on social media:

✓ **DO:** Check on your members, neighbors, and especially those who are elderly, disabled, or vulnerable in other ways.

✗ **DON'T:** Self-deploy as a volunteer, especially during the search and rescue phase. You will only get in the way or put yourself in danger.

✓ **DO:** If there are needs in your congregation and you belong to a national denomination, please contact your Regional Office, District Superintendent, or appropriate middle judicatory office, so they can coordinate ways to provide support through available disaster funds and organizations.

✓ **DO:** Check with your local VOAD (Volunteer Organizations Active in Disaster) about needs of survivors before collecting any material donations.

✗ **DON'T:** Collect material donations without arranging an appropriate destination (local social service agency, etc.).

✓ **DO:** Know that money is the most flexible donation you can make. Denominational and other disaster response funds often have really low overhead and are efficient, effective ways to turn your generosity into assistance.

✓ **DO:** If eligible, encourage all affected folks in your congregation and community to apply to FEMA for Federal Disaster Assistance. Please be aware that this is a long process, and be sure to read all documents carefully. An initial rejection does not mean one cannot appeal; an applicant may also be eligible for low-interest loans to replace damaged property.

✗ **DON'T:** Get discouraged by how long the process takes.

✓ **DO:** Become familiar with FEMA's sequence of delivery. (http://www.fema.gov/pdf/about/regions/regioni/sequence2008.pdf)

✗ **DON'T:** Organize material good distributions that might compromise an affected person's eligibility for aid. (Let the sequence of delivery be your guide.)

✓ **DO:** Encourage leaders in your congregations to become involved in the formation of a long- term recovery committee and to put their skills to work.

✓ **DO:** Stay hopeful. Recovery takes a long time, even among well-supported, well-organized communities.

21

Good News in the Face of Bad News

A Bible Study for Groups and Individuals

Let's face it. We live in an age of bad news—close to home, and far way. Unfiltered media access to footage of droughts, hurricanes, earthquakes, tsunamis, wild fires, civil wars, and intractable poverty brings disaster into our living rooms and lives. As people of faith, we may not be fully equipped to interpret or responsibly respond to the magnitude of human suffering and devastation we encounter through the media. It also may be difficult for us to comprehend the potential for long-term transformation of our communities, for better and for worse, after a disaster.

What does good news look like in the face of the bad news that perpetually interrupts and challenges our faith? This study explores biblical disasters and aims to help churches think constructively about God's involvement in transforming the bad news of the world into a gospel of good news for all God's suffering people. It will help your congregation to interpret and respond to the "expected unexpected" events in your pastoral, mission, and outreach ministries.

Pastors and church leaders don't preach, teach, or speak about death only at funerals, or love only at weddings, or grace only at a baptism. Neither should we wait to deal with the threat or reality of a disaster only when an emergency floods our hearts or a crisis quakes our faith.

Bonnie Osei-Frimpong has worked with Week of Compassion, Church World Service Indonesia, and the American Red Cross. Bonnie is committed to the ecumenical Church and sustainable communities. She lives in Chicago with her family.

Disasters of Biblical Proportion?

The biblical paradigm for disaster is often assumed to be that the sovereign God of Creation will create and destroy at will, as with the establishment of the earth in seven days and the Great Flood that wipes most of it out. According to the psalmist, God uses divine, nature-bending power to establish fear and awe: "May the glory of the LORD endure forever; / may the LORD rejoice in his works— / who looks on the earth and it trembles, / who touches the mountains and they smoke" (Ps. 104:31–32, NRSV). There are instances in the Bible where God is portrayed as using disasters to punish communities who violate the commandments or neglect the Covenant, as with the destruction of Sodom and Gomorrah (Gen. 19) and the twelve plagues of Egypt (Ex. 5—12). Other times, a disaster allows God's people to be faithful and wise, and to prevent calamity, as with Joseph's interpretation of Pharaoh's dream of coming drought and famine (Gen. 41).

The term "disaster of biblical proportions" is consistently assumed to be synonymous with the most profound incidents of death and destruction in all of human experience. However, such a reading of biblical disasters is much too narrow. A more expansive review of biblical disasters teaches us about God's deep and abiding relationship with all that God created and called "good" and "very good," and especially about the God who is with us "always, even to the end of the age" (Mt. 28:20, NASB). Studying stories of disasters in the Bible reinforces God's deep commitment to and compassion for all who suffer, and God's continual re-creation and transformation of the broken places in our lives and world.

Several selections of scripture follow, along with notes and five guiding questions. This study could be utilized by a Sunday school class interested in discussing a single scripture over a number of weeks, an individual spending a week or longer reflecting on each scripture, or a larger cross-section of a congregation or other group interested in dividing into small groups with each group taking on a scripture, spending time exploring and discussing, then sharing with the larger group.

SESSION 1

Scripture: Psalm 22 (NRSV)

FOR STUDY _____

One of the great spiritual challenges confronting survivors of and witnesses to a disaster is just to express what happened to them and how they feel about it. "There are no words" is often the most honest expression of both trauma and empathy. It is not the case that communicating confusion and pain is useless, but that it is impossible to explain what happened or justify the complex whirl of doubt, grief, anger, guilt, and fear, among other emotions, that a devastating trauma can cause.

Well-intentioned people often resort to platitudes and clichés such as "Everything happens for a reason," or, "God knows best." These expressions can sound meaningless and empty. To someone who has experienced trauma, it would be liberating to know that he or she is not the only one who has survived a horrific experience that no one should have to endure.

Fortunately the Scriptures are a rich resource for spiritual solace, even in the face of a devastating disaster, in part because they help survivors or witnesses find the weighty words to articulate their experience. Psalm 22 reads like a welcome sympathy card for someone traumatized by disaster. It begins with words that Jesus himself borrowed at the darkest hours of his life: "My God, my God, why have you forsaken me? / Why are you so far from helping me, from the words of my groaning? (v. 1). In verse 14, "I am poured out like water, / and all my bones are out of joint; / my heart is like wax, / it is melted within my breast..." And yet, the psalmist continues to sing, "For [you] did not despise.../ the affliction of the afflicted; / [you] did not hide [your] face from me, / but heard when I cried to [you]" (v. 24).

Psalm 22 unflinchingly acknowledges the uncomfortable spiritual truths that accompany loss, but does so in a way that upholds God's goodness and mercy. Read to a victim in need of solace, or used as a litany or prayer in a worship service, Psalm 22 could be an affirming and healing spiritual aid that also communicates to others the mystery and profundity of loss.

FOR FURTHER REFLECTION _____

1. What disaster(s) is/are presented in the text?
2. Do you think about this text differently when you focus especially on the disaster?
3. Does the disaster affect your understanding of what is at stake in the text?
4. What insights might be drawn that relate to understanding God, humankind, Creation, Church, etc.?
5. How could this text be useful in preaching, counseling, advising, and teaching about God's enduring love for Creation?

SESSION II

Scripture: Psalm 46 (NRSV)

FOR STUDY

Individuals experience disaster in the midst of their community and culture. Cities and whole societies are affected when a disaster occurs. Psalm 46 reminds the faithful that creating a community and culture that trusts in God's justice and faithfulness is the best preparation for natural disaster or political unrest: "Therefore we will not fear, though the earth should change, / though the mountains shake in the heart of the sea" (v. 2). But for all the traditions of the past and plans for the future that they embody, the psalm reinforces that human institutions, run by politics and economics, are not as enduring as God's laws, nor as inevitable as God's righteousness: "The nations are in an uproar, the kingdoms totter; / he utters his voice, the earth melts... / The God of Jacob is our refuge" (v. 6, 7b).

This passage expressly deals with earthquakes, tsunami, social strife, and warfare, and how a God-fearing community fortifies itself in the face of natural disaster and political turmoil. The psalm's first stanza establishes the bottom line for this community: " God is our refuge and our strength, / a very present help in trouble." When peace and prosperity are interrupted, the psalmist credits God with the desolation: " Come, behold the works of the LORD; / see what desolations he has brought to the earth" (v. 8). Meanwhile, the community observes that God's involvement "makes wars cease to the end of the earth; / he breaks the bow, and shatters the spear; / he burns the shields with fire" (v. 9). God has moved to establish a new kind of creation.

Not all disasters hearken a better world coming, but this psalm reveals a powerful spiritual lesson—that although the timing of God's interaction with the world is impossible to predict, the characteristic outcome, the mark of God's righteousness, is revealed in the transformation of suffering into steadfast mercy and peace. Although we cannot ignore the pangs of suffering, among people or within Creation, we hold fast to our faithful God who will provide a meaning and purpose out of the baffling succession of unpredictable events.

FOR FURTHER REFLECTION

1. What disaster(s) is/are presented in the text?
2. Do you think about this text differently when you focus especially on the disaster it depicts?
3. Does the disaster affect your understanding of what is at stake in the text?

4. What insights might be drawn that relate to understanding God, humankind, Creation, Church, etc.?

5. How could this text be useful in preaching, counseling, advising, and teaching about God's enduring love for Creation?

SESSION III

Scripture: Acts 16:25–39 (NRSV)

FOR STUDY

The earthquake that opens the gates of the prison where Paul and Timothy are detained is only the most obvious disaster in this passage. Another disaster is the clear rupture of the systems of Roman justice, in their courts and prisons. Paul and Timothy have broken no law and ought not to be in prison; but they are jailed by judges who bend to the will of the mob rather than human or divine laws. In prison, Paul and Timothy worship late into the night, when an earthquake destroys the jailhouse.

Realizing the prisoners have become unchained, the prison guard prepares to take his own life. Death at his own hand is better than the punishment his supervisors will inflict when they realize the prisoners escaped. But in the story's most unexpected turn, Paul and Timothy announce: "Do not harm yourself, for we are all here." (v. 28).

Rather than succumbing to the anger and frustration of the moral disaster of unjust imprisonment, and rather than panicking in the trauma of a natural disaster, Paul and Timothy testify to God's transformative truth—their surest confidence in a world of uncertainty.

The first shock people of faith may find in Paul and Timothy's example is that faithfulness works in profoundly unpredictable and transformative ways. Although they are unjustly imprisoned, and although the prison falls down around them, Paul is never distracted from trusting God and witnessing to Christ's truth. This not only limits the scope of the disaster, it actively allows God's transformation to take hold in a crisis situation. Their example contrasts with the temptation we all face to allow anger at injustice or shock at a crisis overwhelm our faithful witness. Paul and Timothy helpfully demonstrate that trusting God can appear foolish, but, even amid deadly destruction, being faithful to God's ways and truths is profoundly effective, even when we do not know what else to do.

The disasters in this story reveal the power of mercy to release, redeem, restore, and revive survivors and witnesses of trauma. Instead of excusing themselves from captivity at the first opportunity, Paul and Timothy remain long enough to release their captor from his fear and failures. They then welcome his whole family into the church. They go on to model the brokenness of the institutional structures that betrayed them in the first place, by insisting on justice and dignity from the judges, guards, and political officials involved in their detention. Their survival skills and faithful witness establish the real possibility of justice and life in a broken political system and an earthquake-rattled city.

FOR FURTHER REFLECTION

1. What disaster(s) is/are presented in the text?
2. Do you think about this text differently when you focus especially on the disaster?
3. Does the disaster affect your understanding of what is at stake in the text?
4. What insights might be drawn that relate to understanding God, humankind, Creation, Church, etc.?
5. How could this text be useful in preaching, counseling, advising, and teaching about God's enduring love for Creation?

SESSION IV

Scripture: Acts 27:13–44

FOR STUDY

Everything that can go wrong does on Paul's journey to the emperor in Rome to plead his case. The storm season has arrived, but the ship's captain is more concerned with protecting the investors and their investments aboard the boat than the 276 passengers and crew. Their journey demonstrates how our mislaid priorities, values, and fears can lead disastrous situations to go from bad to worse, clouding our judgment and endangering ourselves and others in vulnerable situations.

Paul's vessel and voyage both seem doomed. They encounter high winds, rough seas, rocky shores, and no hope for escape. As the ship flounders in the tempest, which is a lot like a hurricane or cyclone, the seamen throw their valuable cargo overboard. Next they dump the bait, and their prospects for survival fade as the likelihood of starvation grows. In the midst of the crisis, Paul offers them the good news/bad news of practical, faith-filled wisdom, saying essentially: "You should have listened to me before so listen to me now." An angel had announced to him in prayer that all the boats and goods will be lost, but, by holding together and staying courageous they all would survive (v. 21–23).

Paul anticipated that the ship would run aground, destroying any remaining cargo. But he demonstrates that the dignity of human life is far more precious than the captain's misplaced pride and the goods on the boat. He models faithfulness and courage in the face of destruction and doom, and saves many lives in the process. Most significantly and more subtly, though, Paul shows that courage-filled faithfulness is more precious to God than merely surviving hard times. It wasn't just about surviving this disastrous voyage, but also about creating a way to live through the uncertainty, to transform the lives of others by Paul's own faithful witness. Paul's example creates small ripples of faith and hope in the hearts of the voyagers, prisoners, and, later, among the barbarians on the isle of Malta, which no tempest could trouble.

FOR FURTHER REFLECTION

1. What disaster(s) is/are presented in the text?
2. Do you think about this text differently when you focus especially on the disaster?
3. Does the disaster affect your understanding of what is at stake in the text?
4. What insights might be drawn that relate to understanding God, humankind, Creation, Church, etc.?
5. How could this text be useful in preaching, counseling, advising, and teaching about God's enduring love for Creation?

SESSION V

Scripture: Acts 28:1–6

FOR STUDY

Paul deals with one thing after another on this seemingly doomed voyage to Rome. After fourteen days adrift, facing starvation, shipwrecked off Malta, preserving the lives of passenger and crew, swimming to shore, and seeking shelter and aid, Paul still doesn't catch a break. In this next adventure, he engages responsibly in a ministry of compassion to other people who have endured a disaster.

The islanders of Malta show the shipwrecked strangers unusual kindness (v. 2). This is noteworthy because they don't speak the same languages or follow Roman laws. Considering that the Maltese had weathered the same brutal storm on land that the voyagers faced at sea, we can assume that their houses, crops, and families had not survived intact. The Maltese could have responded with violence or apathy to these needy, frightened, hungry, and vulnerable strangers in their midst.

Instead, they cooperated to gather wood for a fire, to dry off, warm up, cook, and rejuvenate. In the midst of this useful model of partnership, Paul, still shackled with handcuffs and iron chains, is bitten by a viper. The islanders conclude that Paul is a murderer or a wizard, but when he does not die from the poisonous snake, they decide he must be a god. The Maltese are ready to worship and revere him for his good luck, his good health, and his good heart.

But for Paul, that is exactly the wrong response. Paul is a follower of Jesus Christ, not for the sake of his own good or glory, but because he deeply believes the transformative truth of the gospel. To him, everything else is either a distraction or an opportunity to preach the gospel, even when it costs him comfort and security. This story indicates the persistent "one thing after another" frustrations that disasters cause, and especially reveals our own tendency to want to serve as semi-saviors when others are in need.

Being rooted in a mature faith, Paul redirects the emphasis outward from himself and toward God and others who are vulnerable and suffering.

FOR FURTHER REFLECTION

1. What disaster(s) is/are presented in the text?
2. Do you think about this text differently when you focus especially on the disaster?
3. Does the disaster affect your understanding of what is at stake in the text?
4. What insights might be drawn that relate to understanding God, humankind, Creation, Church, etc.?
5. How could this text be useful in preaching, counseling, advising, and teaching about God's enduring love for Creation?

SESSION VI

Scripture: Matthew 28

FOR STUDY

The grieving women at Jesus' tomb have survived spiritual whiplash in the traumatic days and hours that have just passed. One week earlier, Jesus had marched into Jerusalem and the crowds shouted "Hosanna!" But then, a few days later, this King was crucified. The world had turned the disciples' highest hopes and most sacred beliefs into something to laugh about. Jesus, the one that they hoped would restore the Temple, end the injustice, fix the corruption, heal the sick, and put food on the table, had been put to death—just when real progress was starting.

To top it off, as the women are weeping, there is an earthquake so powerful that they can't see or hear anything! The guards fall down in fear, like dead men (v. 4). An angel appears, announcing that Jesus is raised. The women can't believe what they are seeing and hearing, yet they are told to announce the good news.

It's a disastrously ambivalent moment for the women, who are rightfully overcome by fear. It is hard to decide if what they have heard is good news or bad news. They are either devastated or overjoyed, but they don't know which. Verse 8 says they are terrified and amazed. Even though a disaster causes confusion and fear, it also makes our most important priorities easier to identify.

The angel in Mathew's gospel is a messenger. The word for "angels" in Greek literally means "bearers of good news," or "witnesses." This angel tells the women two things: Jesus is alive, and don't be afraid. For the women, this sounds like too little too late. Didn't they really need the angels a few days earlier?

But actually the role this angelic witness plays cannot be overestimated. He remained with the grieving women throughout the crisis, and stayed after, too. The angel models for the Church that to witness disastrous suffering is a hard, holy task. The most faithful response to the profound suffering of others involves allowing ourselves to enter into their grief.

The angel's presence with the women at the tomb turns us into witnesses who see and proclaim, as did the women—fearfully and with great joy—that the bad news of a disaster can be transformed to good news for the world. With this witness to seismic compassion, we are invited to feel fully alive, fragile, and incarnated.

FOR FURTHER REFLECTION

1. What disaster(s) is/are presented in the text?
2. Do you think about this text differently when you focus especially on the disaster?
3. Does the disaster affect your understanding of what is at stake in the text?
4. What insights might be drawn that relate to understanding God, humankind, Creation, Church, etc.?
5. How could this text be useful in preaching, counseling, advising, and teaching about God's enduring love for Creation?

22

Sample Resources for Post-Disaster Worship

On January 12, 2010, the worst natural disaster in Haiti's history happened. An earthquake rocked the tiny island nation and in a matter of mere minutes hundreds of thousands of peoples' lives changed. Bombarded by heart-wrenching images of the aftermath of the earthquake, many people across North America and the world were moved to respond. One of our most important responses to disaster, as faith communities, is worship. These sample litanies could easily be adapted to other disaster scenarios.

LITANY 1 FOR WORSHIP

BONNIE OSEI-FRIMPONG

ONE: God witnesses the wounded in places of need around the world.
MANY: God whispers, "kenbe fem," my Haitian children. "***Hold strong***."
ONE: God listens to thirsty children carrying buckets to the well.
MANY: God sings with them, "kinywaji," my Congolese children. "***Drink it in.***"
ONE: God understands the widowed mother rocking her sleeping child.
MANY: God holds them both and says, "Ja sam s vama." "***I am with you,***" in Bosnia and in the world.
ONE: We worship "God with us," in whose love we serve.
ALL: Thanks be to God.

LITANY 2 FOR WORSHIP

ONE: God, you did not come to destroy life, but to save it.
MANY: We trust in your everlasting love.

ONE: It is not the end of the world. But for your beloved people in Haiti, it is the end of the world they have known.

MANY: Our quaking hearts are moved in a new direction, with a strength and urgency your faithful have known before.

ONE: You call us to merciful justice. You call us to courageous compassion. You call us to hope. We will answer your call.

ALL: Set our lives in this direction: to serve all that you created and called "good." Amen.

OFFERING INVITATION

Disasters create a challenge and an opportunity for the Church. When earthquakes, hurricanes, or tsunamis interrupt our normal lives, we wonder why God allows natural disasters to happen. Why didn't God stop it? Where is God? Compassionate people ask, "What can I do to help?"

Our faith compels us to keep asking questions. In the Church we don't find the complete answers, but we do find faith, hope, and love, which help us endure. We believe God created the world and called it good. We believe God is with us. We believe God knows all our needs and hears all our cries.

The Church helps us to love our neighbors more, *and* to love them *better*. We are touched by love in preparing plastic bags with fingernail files and bandages, to help bodies that are hurt and hearts that are broken. In our outreach for Haiti, we will "pay, pray, and stay" until the time is right, when we will "go, grow, and know."

We thank God that, as a Church, we rise with courageous compassion to the challenge and opportunity disasters create.

INVITATION TO COMMUNION

REV. JOHNNY WRAY

In the aftermath of the earthquake in Haiti, the words from the first Corinthian letter speak with a new urgency, a new vitality, a new reality. "If one member suffers, all suffer together...; if one member rejoices, all rejoice together" Indeed it seems as if the whole world has been in suffering solidarity with the people of Haiti; anguishing and weeping with them as the death toll continues to rise; as aid never seems to reach the need soon enough; as personal tragic story after personal tragic story is displayed daily in our dens and family rooms. And yet there are those moments of triumph and rejoicing—a baby rescued after days trapped in the rubble; a small Haitian relief organization found quietly and effectively caring for scores and scores of quake survivors; rescue and aid workers from every corner of the world carrying out their duties...

These same words provided their own personal poignancy to me as two friends and formers colleagues were killed in the collapse of the Hotel Montana, and now two widows grieve and children are fatherless; while two other good friends and former colleagues were rescued and are now safely back home, reunited with their families.

Sometimes the tension of this suffering together and this rejoicing together is overwhelming, yet it is indelibly held together.

And, of course, no place more so than at this Table. Here we remember, we share the suffering of Christ—his rejection, his pain, his death, and at the same time we also celebrate and rejoice in Christ's triumph over sin and death.

These are the gifts of God for the people of God.

A PRAYER FOR THE VICTIMS OF VIOLENT WATERS

AMY GOPP

God of Hope and Healing,

The suffering seems too great, the devastation caused by hurricanes and tsunamis too vast. We have been bombarded by images of death and destruction caused by the violent forces of [*Hurricanes Katrina and Rita and the tsunamis in Asia*], yet we are often left looking instead of responding. How do we respond to such tragedy? How do we continue to trust in your healing power when such loss occurs in the world?

Nevertheless, just as you were present during the parting of the Sea of Reeds, the calming of the storms and waters, and the curing of the sick and afflicted, so you are present during these crises. We may not understand how you are working in the midst of such anguish, but we trust you are there, as you have been and always will be. You are The Great I Am. You are the One who tames the seas.

We are not used to disasters of this magnitude affecting our own people. Grant us the wisdom to know how to continue to pray for all those affected by [*Katrina, Rita, and Wilma*] and so many other water disasters. Open our hearts and homes that we may offer hospitality and compassion. May Christ's healing balm soothe the souls and bodies of all those whose lives have been turned upside down by this tragedy.

Yes, the suffering seems too great, but your everlasting love, abounding grace, and healing power is even greater.

In this we trust and believe. May these convictions inspire us further as we respond to our sisters and brothers in need.

Amen.

SAMPLE PASTORAL PRAYER

Amy Gopp

Gracious, gracious God,

Here we are.

We come before you on this Sabbath day to worship you, and you alone. We come to seek your mercy. We come to experience your unconditional love. We come to you to ask for guidance and courage as we strive to be people of peace; people who love others so deeply that our love helps to heal the world you have entrusted to us. We come with a longing in our hearts—for our world, for our community, for this church, for our families, and for our own lives.

Listen now, God of Comfort, to our earnest prayers, shared now in silent meditation: [*silence*].

You are the God who hears our prayers. You are the God who is always there, present, working in our lives and moving throughout our midst. Even when it may *seem* that you have not heard our cries, when it may *seem* as though you have not answered our prayers, may we learn to understand and accept your response even when it may not be what we would have wanted or expected. Grant us faith. We beseech you to be patient with us when we have not heard you or have not allowed *you* to be God. We surrender all. Right here, right now, we surrender our fears, our hopes, our longings, our pain, our work, our relationships, our anxieties; our very lives we surrender to you.

Cradle us in your arms of tender loving care, and remind us that you are with us during disaster, in crisis, in sickness, through trauma, and even upon death. Embrace us as we deal with loss, with the pain of endings and the grief of destruction and death, and guide us as we look to new beginnings and fresh ideas. Strengthen us as this body, part of *the* Body of our Lord Jesus Christ, so that we are able to love and care for one another in an authentic way. May this loving care empower us to spread your love to the entire world. Every end of the earth is in dire need of your unconditional acceptance and love. Hold our hands as we take risks and move outside of our comfort zones, not simply as a passive body waiting for you to act but intentionally calling upon you to act through us, with us, around us, and within us. For we know that we have been called—chosen—to act in response to what you have already done and continue to do in our individual lives and in the life of this community of faith.

So walk with us now as we reach out [*to the people of Newtown who are reeling from senseless violence in their community; to Haitians still recovering from a vicious earthquake; to Congolese in the midst of war; to Americans along the East Coast affected by Superstorm Sandy and in Moore, Oklahoma, struggling to rebuild their homes, find new jobs, and reconstruct their communities after the devastating tornado;*] to all those who have lost jobs here at home; to those who have no home to go to; to all of us seated here, for our families and our joys and concerns... We pray specifically for [*READ PRAYER LIST*]. We surrender all to you.

Lord God, these are the desires and prayers of our hearts. We know that you hear these prayers and that you are in constant conversation with us. Indeed, hear us, O Lord, as we join together in unison as we say the prayer Jesus taught us to pray, saying, "Our Father." (*Congregation is invited to join leader in Lord's Prayer.*)

Amen.

One Great Hour to Share

(See next page for sheet music.)

You celebrate my glory in the beauty of the earth,
In love that brings forgiveness, in the miracle of birth.
You offer up your gratitude in worship and in prayer.
But what I really want from you is willingness to share.

REFRAIN

>When the wind and the rain of the hurricane left me homeless on the street,
>Did you give me clothes and shelter, Did you bring me food to eat?
>When the warlords came and I fled the flames,
>When they made me a refugee,
>Did you feel my racing heart beat? Hear my cries of agony?
>When the heat and the sand of this barren land left me struggling to survive,
>Did you help me find clean water, so my family could thrive?
>When I was lost and lonely, and wandering in despair,
>My greatest time of need was your one great hour to share.

The questions you can't answer that keep you up at night:
Why evil strikes the innocent and darkness rules the light.
On the day when every eye can see, when all accounts are squared,
the question that will matter most is: "Did they know you cared?"

REFRAIN

My world for all its beauty, can be an ugly place.
Suffering comes, and hopes and dreams vanish without trace.
Though tragedy can bring on pain you simply can't erase,
It gives each soul a chance to be an instrument of grace.

REFRAIN

Steve Gretz is an ordained minister in the American Baptist Churches and serves as pastor of the Greece Baptist Church in Rochester, N.Y. Involved in music most of his life, Steve has been seriously performing and recording since the 1990s. A talented graphic designer, Leslie Lee has grown as a singer since she first stepped behind the microphone to record *Recovered* with Steve in 2003. More of their music is available at www.leslieandsteve.com.

One Great Hour To Share

Leslie Lee &
Steve Gretz

23

Being Loved, the Ultimate Hope

Preaching Following a Disaster

SEUNG (PAUL) TCHE

Does the Bible directly teach us how to respond or react to natural or human-made disasters? I wish that I could answer this question with an unequivocal yes, but the answer is much more complicated. As human beings, we long to comprehend the things that happen to us. Everything happens for a reason, we often say. We would like to know why we have been hit by a disaster, and, often, religions are great resources for answers to our "big" questions. It is relatively easy to find theological explanations, pseudoscientific religious analyses, and even shamanistic approaches about these incomprehensible situations. Answering these questions with both pastoral and prophetic integrity, however, requires a more nuanced approach. It is to this task that those who preach to communities affected by disasters are called.

In my understanding, the most dangerous way to react to a disaster such as a hurricane or earthquake is to name the disaster as an example of how God rages against human sin. Many prophets and preachers have tried to convince others that everything has a reason, and, many times, the reasons they give for those disasters is that they are warnings or punishments from God for our sinful behavior.

Here is our question, then: Do we really believe that God would use naturally caused or even human-made disasters to discipline God's

---

Seung (Paul) Tche serves as pastor of White Oak Pond Christian Church in Richmond, Kentucky. A committed ecumenist, he serves as chair of the board of the Council for Christian Unity for the Christian Church (Disciples of Christ) and as a member of the Week of Compassion Advisory Committee.

own people? Is that our Christian faith? What about the God who has made promises through Noah? The Scripture says, "[God] will never again curse the ground because of humankind, for the inclination of the human heart is evil from youth; nor will I ever again destroy every living creature as I have done" (Gen. 8:21, NRSV). Nonetheless, there are some Christians who believe that disasters are caused by our sinfulness. If that is the case, unfortunately, we believe in a God who harasses the innocent and the guilty alike through those fearful events. Or, we theologically justify why the innocent also have to suffer from the consequences of others' sinful actions: because we all are born in original sin.

I know that many contemporary preachers never preach this kind of theology from the pulpit when a disaster hits. While everyone might not agree with this kind of understanding about disasters, it is worthwhile to ask why people easily fall into this rather unenlightened attempt to comprehend disasters. First, perhaps it is because of fear that there might be another disaster to come, and, by knowing why, we can either prevent one or create a framework for understanding and accept the fact that disasters are also part of our human life. Second, where despair prevails and infects every bit of life, it is hard to justify the existence of a good, loving God. According to this line of thinking, preachers often imagine a God who uses disaster to discipline for the good of the world, and we are left to believe that there is hope behind the actions of an angry, violent God.

The more we engage this kind of understanding of disasters, the more our ideas and conversations about God and a life of faith become inhumane. Suddenly, God becomes only a controlling God who is either distant and removed from our suffering, or complicit in it. We want to believe that, even though we are suffering from the effects of a disaster, hope and comfort come from the fact that God is in control. Surely, there is a sense of security when we know that our suffering is part of the big picture of God's control. But is it a sound understanding of our suffering from a disaster? Is there a real hope behind this understanding? Is it really comfort?

When engaging communities affected by disasters, another tactic that preachers too easily utilize is creating some virtual reality of tomorrow. We would like to assure our congregations that there is a brighter, easier future, and that we will rise from the ashes of today and build a brand new tomorrow. While a message of hope is something that people really need to hear from the pulpit, this message can offer false promises, or ignore the notion that a congregation needs to be resilient and participate in their community's recovery.

If members of a congregation have to face long-term recovery, or if they face only massive destruction and death, a hoped-for tomorrow may seem elusive. In this case, our promise for tomorrow extends to another reality in God in the future: the New Jerusalem—where God will dwell with the mortals and where there are no tears, no death, no mourning or crying, and no pain (Rev. 21:3–4)—is waiting for us.

I also know that many preachers would never preach this kind of blindly beautiful future, either. But disasters can change everything, even the behaviors and understandings we have previously cultivated. When we are confronted by death, we might find ourselves offering the New Jerusalem. When hardships of life hit us really hard, we have a tendency to ignore facing the reality of today and put a tremendous amount of hope into God's Kingdom in the afterlife.

Our faith in God, however, always asks us to face today and to move toward tomorrow. There is hope for tomorrow without abandoning today. What our Christian faith challenges us to do is face reality even if it is very hard to do. God asks us to open our eyes and to look around us once again.

Even though the Scriptures don't explicitly teach us how to respond to natural or human-made disasters, the Scriptures show us how to bring God's hope for a time when there are no more tears into the current harsh reality. The stories that span Genesis to Revelation tell us that God's hope, God's reconciling work, God's future does not only exist in some temporal future but also permeates through today's life. In order to make God's future visible today, a congregation needs courage to meet life head-on first.

And that takes hope!

The key question for preachers in the midst or aftermath of disaster, thus, is to preach about hope in the midst of despair. How can we preach a sermon that can strengthen individuals and community? How can we preach about hope without justifying disasters as God's rage or without creating a false reality for today and tomorrow? Surely, this is a big task.

No matter how we understand who God is, as Christians there is no doubt that in every circumstance of our lives the source from which hope streams is God. But our challenge is that it is not easy to point out where we can find God's hope in the midst of a disaster. To many, God observes humanity from a distance; God's hands are never dirty from disaster cleanup. To many people in areas of disasters, God seems distant, even absent. There is no divine breath, only that of the darkness itself. Only despair befriends destruction.

Another crucial task of a preacher in the midst of or after a disaster is to point to God's presence, as elusive as it may be. I have found the Lazarus story to be a powerful tool for pointing to the presence of divine hope. In the story, we understand that Jesus wept with those who wept when they were distraught by loss of the loved one. God, present in the ministry of Jesus, is right here among the suffering. The story reminds us that God is with us at our most vulnerable—when we are grief-stricken, angry, and feeling utterly abandoned. When Martha turned on Jesus in anger, Jesus showed her compassion. When Martha, Mary, and other people grieved, Jesus stood among them, greatly disturbed by their inconsolable grief. Lazarus is raised from the dead, but that's not the ultimate point of the story. The point is that God loves us, and God's love is great enough to swallow up death forever. God's love is strong enough to sustain our lives here on earth even if the dark shadow of death is prevailing. God's love is open enough to accept our grief and anger. God's love is full of hope for tomorrow. Tomorrow, of course, belongs to God.

The ultimate hope for people when they are devastated rests on the reminder that they are cared for and loved; that they are not alone; that their prayers are heard. Maybe, at the moment, the only message that they need to hear from the pulpit is that God is suffering with them. The fact that God and they share pain together will enable people to carry on; even though the future may have its own challenges, God's hope remains. It is the task of the preacher to be the voice who reminds God's people that mountains may crumble, but God isn't going anywhere.

24

Constructing a Sermon on Disasters

Brandon Gilvin

I preach about disasters a lot.

As part of my work with a denominational mission fund for disaster response, refugee resettlement, and global development, I am often invited into congregations to share about the work that we do in partnership with the Church and our partners from all over the world. Our congregations are diverse, made up of people with a variety of opinions, different perspectives on the role of God in the world, and a range of experiences with disasters large and small— often, very personal.

Given my call to this work, I've spent a lot of time thinking about how to preach about disasters in a way that is theologically responsible, provides insight into some of the "best practices" of disaster response, ties the work that we do as a mission fund to God's redemptive work in the world, and hopefully inspires listeners to see our work as part of *their* calling as well. In doing so, I've developed a few interpretive strategies and structural habits that have proven helpful.

Preaching is a craft, and I've leaned on the work of colleagues, mentors, and writers and artists in all sorts of mediums to find ways to forge something that works for me. Some of these strategies might work for you; you may have other ideas that prove to be better tools.

Preach the Gospel

While there are many good, fair, ethical ways to speak about disasters, there is a difference between giving a speech about a disaster and preaching

---

Brandon Gilvin serves as Associate Director of Week of Compassion, the disaster and development fund of the Christian Church (Disciples of Christ).

153

the Gospel. To preach the Gospel is to proclaim the Reign of God (Mk. 1:14–15; Mt. 4:17): the hope that one day all people will be reconciled, all that has been damaged will be restored (Lk. 4:17–21), and that the priorities of an often violent world will be turned upside down (Mt. 5.1—7:29; Lk. 6:20–49).[54] The Gospel is an invitation to see peace where there is war, food where there is hunger, and hope where there is nothing.

A sermon, therefore, invites its hearers into an imaginative act: locating our story in the vision of a coming Reign of reconciliation, peace, and hope for the suffering. For a person of faith, disaster response is more than just a technical endeavor, and a well-executed response is more than just a job well done. It is holy work. A disaster site, filled with the stories of loss and recovery, is holy ground.

For people of faith, most of the key metaphors, images, and stories that shape the notions of what is holy—what the Reign of God looks like—come from scripture. Weaving a sense of how holy the work of disaster recovery is into one's sense of the holy means making connections between scripture and the stories we tell. Making those connections requires not only imagination, but also a little research.

Historical Context Is Your Friend

The Bible is full of stories of disaster. Inviting a congregation to experience a selection from scripture as a rich, powerful story requires understanding some of the historical and social contexts involved. The more you know, the easier it is to make connections to contemporary experiences of disaster. As I've spent time studying and preparing, several scriptures have emerged as rich resources for preaching the Gospel; the more I've learned about their context, the better.

Some examples:

- The Book of Lamentations and Jeremiah. At the heart of these books is the Babylonian conquest of Jerusalem in 586 B.C.E. and the exile that followed. Few events in the Bible are as disastrous, and the poetry of both Lamentations and Jeremiah evokes both powerful grief and resilient hope.
- Exodus. The rich stories of escaped slaves, oppression at the hands of a superpower, and a wandering, rag-tag multitude helps elucidate the experience of those displaced by violent, human-caused disaster.
- Luke 6:17–23 and Acts 2:43–47. This is a great combination of scriptures for a number of reasons. Most scholars assume that there's a historical connection between the two books—perhaps written by the same author(s)—and they serve as great examples

of Jesus' vision of the Reign of God and how the early church attempted to live into that vision. The image in Acts 2:44–45 of the early disciples sharing their resources "as any had need" speaks powerfully to how we might respond to those affected by natural and human-caused disasters.

If preaching is not something you do regularly, or you have not attended seminary, that's fine. While it's important to responsibly interpret scripture and represent its context as accurately as possible, preaching is not the same thing as teaching a graduate seminar on an ancient text. Listeners can only digest so much history, and keep track of so many dates. Using good scholarly commentaries or even a well-written Study Bible will provide great, concise information that will help you. The Bible study included in this toolkit is a great resource, too.

To help a congregation dive into the scripture, I will often note a couple of things that I want them to listen for *before* I read the scripture, rather than interpreting a text or explaining a fine point in the middle of a sermon. This seems to help people make the connections between ancient scripture and contemporary story, and helps the sermon itself flow better. I keep this section very brief (30–120 seconds) and then read the scripture immediately after and, most importantly, I tell the congregation what I'm doing. For example:

Before I dive into the scripture this morning, I'd like to spend a little time "setting the scene."

This morning's scripture reading comes from the book of Lamentations, which is a collection of songs, poems, and prayers in response to one of the most devastating events in the history of ancient Israel.

In 586 B.C.E., the Babylonian empire—the superpower of the day—conquered Jerusalem and destroyed the temple—the center of religious, political, and social life—and hauled off Jerusalem's best and brightest to Babylon to live in exile.

In terms of disaster, it's hard to imagine anything more devastating.

But these poems, prayers, and songs also express a deeply embedded hope in a God who covenanted with Hebrew people: a God who promised to be present with them in all things.

It is in their hope that we can learn something about our own response to the disasters that affect us and our neighbors around the world.

Let us open our hearts and open our minds and hear God's word in these words…

Nothing too technical, nothing too scholarly—just basic information about the scripture that helps listeners understand that stories found in scripture are the stories of real people: people as real as those whose contemporary stories of disaster they know, and from which they draw meaning.

Stories Are Parables

According to the Bible, Jesus told great stories. His parables often focused on ordinary, unspectacular things: seeds, candle wicks, brothers who didn't get along, lost sheep. In Jesus' imagination, however, these ordinary events, people, situations, and items pointed toward something else: the Reign of God.

The ordinary becomes extraordinary in a parable by Jesus. Thomas Troeger, who teaches preaching at Yale Divinity School, suggests developing a habit of collecting stories from one's own life as a way of enriching one's own preaching:

> Create parabolic stories or poems, depending on your natural bent as a writer, that have no blatantly religious tone or content but that reveal the truth and meaning of our lives in surprising ways. Save these pieces and periodically review them. You may then discover "the continuous thread of revelation" that would otherwise elude your most strenuous sermonic efforts.[55]

If you have lived through a disaster of any size, you likely have a story that points to some deeper truth, breaks open a new understanding, or has helped you reassign meaning to your life in some way. Perhaps you have been privileged enough to witness the actions of someone else who has brought a sign of grace and hope to an area affected by disaster, even in a tiny way. Even if your story seems ordinary, it has power, especially if you tell it from the heart and with integrity.

What Story Do I Tell?

To preach the Gospel is to tell a story of hope. This doesn't mean that you should whitewash tragedy. Horrible things happen, especially in the midst of disaster. It is important to be honest about that. The psalmists, the author of Lamentations, the prophets, the authors of the Gospels—they described tragedy and disaster, often in graphic ways. However, whether by evoking Israel's covenant or God's Reign, the authors of the Bible understand God as the reservoir of a hope that can be counted upon. There may still be disaster—but disaster is never the final word. Remembering that will help you frame that story.

Second, it's important to remember that you are not the hero of your story. If you were part of a volunteer work group, maybe you did an amazing job putting up drywall. You didn't do that singlehandedly. Even if you built an entire house in a week, your work is part of a bigger effort—of a work group, of a community investing in the long-term recovery process, of a network of donors from around the region, country, or world, of a loving God whose hope is for the reconciliation of all of Creation. The best way you can tell a story is as one bearing witness to a disaster, its recovery, and the hope of a community for a better future.

Third, bear witness to the *dignity* of those affected by disaster. Stories that are constructed to maximize our perception of the suffering of those affected by disaster, and reduce them to flat stereotypes, are exploitive. To simply portray people who are economically vulnerable, from the "Two-thirds World," o very young, or elderly as victims without noting their own agency or resourcefulness may pull at the heartstrings of many a listener, but it does not tell the full story of a community in recovery, nor does it bear witness to the value of an individual as a child of God. Disaster Practitioners with critical eyes refer to this sort of writing as "Disaster Porn" or "Poverty Porn" for a reason. It may seem emotionally gratifying, but it only reduces people and their stories to objects for consumption.

Finally, as Paul Tche states, though it may seem easy or even natural to explain disasters by saying "everything happens for a reason" or describing a disaster as part of God's plan or action for a community or all of humanity, don't do it. The reasons for human suffering—social, psychological, political, and, yes, by way of natural causes—are complex and, in theological terms, mysterious. To quickly assign a cause-and-effect framework that puts the blame on sinful humanity or a micromanaging God is presumptuous at best and cruel at worst. It's not Gospel—it's abuse.

Several years ago, David James Duncan published an essay, "When Compassion Becomes Dissent," which has become for me one of the most important pieces I've ever read on the practice of writing and, by extension, the task of preaching. The work of storytelling, the engagement of the spiritual life, and the ethics we live by as people of faith are, for Duncan, inseparable. When it becomes tempting to sketch out simple answers, or to write something that romanticizes someone's suffering or my role in a community's recovery, I think of his essay:

> To be a Christian, a Buddhist, a Muslim, is to immerse oneself daily in unstinting fiction-making. Christ's words "Love thy neighbor as thyself," to cite a famously ignored example, demand an arduous imaginative act. This deceptively simple line orders me, as I look at you, to imagine that I am not seeing you, but me, and then to treat this imaginative you as if you are me. And for how long? Till the day I die! Christ orders anyone who's serious about him to commit this "Neighbor = Me" fiction until they forget for good which of the two of themselves to cheat in a business deal or abandon in a crisis or smart-bomb in a war—at

which point their imaginative act, their fiction-making, will have turned his words into reality and they'll be saying with Mother Teresa, "I see Christ in every woman and man."[56]

When I visit disaster sites or meet people affected by disaster, I listen for stories of hope. For example, following the 2010 earthquake in Haiti, I met a volunteer who talked about his time there. I've since used his story in my sermon on Lamentations and Disaster:

You notice Raymond as soon as he enters the room.

He's built like a linebacker, but he speaks with a gentle precision that commands your attention: a deliberateness that underscores the fact that he has been admitted to Georgetown Law School.

And you notice that this brilliant, sharp-as-a-tack young man loses just a little bit of his precision when he talks about his time in Haiti.

The son of Haitian immigrants, Raymond took a week's vacation just after the earthquake to serve as a medical translator. Raymond's eyes get misty when he tells you about an old woman lying on a stretcher who reached out to him.

"Are you a doctor?" She asked in Creole.

"No, Ma'am. I am helping translate for the doctors"

She looked puzzled.

"Are you getting paid for that?"

"No, Ma'am."

Another puzzled look.

"Then why are you here?"

"Because, Ma'am, I could help."

The woman held his hand and started stroking it, slowly, as a mother might her own child, and started humming a sad, sweet, yet grateful tune.

A Lament!

"The children of the ones who were forced to leave this place are coming back," she said.

"And they will rebuild this country."

And with that, she went back to humming that sweet, sad thankful tune.

Sharing a story—especially one that is not entirely your own[57]—does come with risks. Do I represent Raymond's experience, the thoughts of an unnamed woman, their interchange, appropriately? Do I exploit her situation, her level of education? I hope not. The search for God's hope in our narratives always requires revision. Get input from colleagues and mentors, trusted friends and family—take their critiques seriously and revise until you tell a story that inspires true hope, not cheap emotional responses.

Final Thoughts

To proclaim the Gospel—at any time—is to proclaim that nothing can separate us from the goodness of God's creation or the love of God. It is to know the ways our sacred stories speak to our situations. It is to record the very real pain that an individual or community has experienced and yet look to the glimpses of shared humanity that break through the rubble or ash. It is to know that the easy answers don't tell the full story, and that embedded in every story is the worth of every person.

Disaster-related preaching requires a specific strategy. This brief essay isn't an exhaustive discussion on how to write a "Disaster sermon," but, hopefully, it serves as a good starting point.

It is most important that you find your own voice. Should your community be affected by a disaster, large or small, your words will have impact. Speak in a way that not only "does no harm," but can inspire the most good.

To preach the Gospel is, after all, to preach "good news," even in the midst of heartbreak.

Notes

Chapter 2: Hurricanes and Lilies

[1]Abraham Joshua Heschel, *The Prophets* (New York: HarperCollins, 2001), 358.

[2]Walter Brueggemann, "Theodicy," in *Reverberations of Faith: A Theological Handbook of Old Testament Themes* (Louisville: Westminster/John Knox, 2002), 213.

[3]Terence E. Fretheim, *Creation Untamed: The Bible, God, and Natural Disasters* (Grand Rapids, Mich.: Baker Academic, 2010), 9ff.

[4]Ibid., 15.

[5]Walter Brueggemann, "A disaster of 'biblical' proportions?" In *Christian Century* (4 October 2005): 23.

[6]Walter Brueggemann, "Chaos," in *Reverberations,* 28.

[7]Aristotle, *Metaphysics,* Book 12; *Physics,* Book 8.

[8]Jürgen Moltmann, *La justicia crea futuro: Política de paz y ética de la creación en un mundo amenazado,* trans. Jesús García-Abril (Santander, Colombia: Editorial Sal Terrae, 1992), 53 (author's translation).

[9]Moltmann, *Cristo para nosotros hoy,* trans. Nancy Bedford (Madrid: Editorial Trotta, 1997), 42 (author's translation).

[10]Ibid., 42–43 (author's translation).

[11]"Statement of Identity of the Christian Church (Disciples of Christ": http://www.disciples.org/21stCenturyVisionTeam/IdentityStatementandPrinciples/tabid/339/Default.aspx.

[12]Valerie Bridgeman Davis, "Retribution as First Response: Did God Punish New Orleans?" *The Sky Is Crying: Race, Class, and Natural Disaster,* ed. Cheryl A. Kirk-Duggan (Nashville: Abingdon Press, 2006), 11.

Chapter 7: Nothing Like That Could Ever Happen Here

[1]You can find out more about *Playmaker* therapy at http://www.lifeisgood.com/playmakers/why.

Chapter 8: Knowing When to Stay and When to Go

[1]Reference to a "Phases of Recovery? – as from Community Arise? –http://www.communityarise.com/course/commresp/commresp/bd_02_01_0090.htm --

[2]The FEMA Sequence of Delivery is found here: https://www.fema.gov/pdf/hazard/wildfire/ca_assist_chart.pdf

[3]See http://www.churchworldservice.org/site/PageServer?pagename=kits_emergency

[4]See "Denominational, Parachurch, and Ecumenical Organizations Involved in Disaster Response ," in chapter 20.

Chapter 9: The Long Term Recovery Process and Your Faith Community

[1]These "4 Cs" are the core principles of the National Voluntary Organizations Active in Disaster (NVOAD), expressed by its many member organizations as they live out their commitment to work together to help communities recover.

[2]*Long Term Recovery Guide,* NVOAD, Dec. 2012, 3 (see also 16). The *Guide* cites a draft of the *National Disaster Recovery Framework,* FEMA, Feb. 5, 2010, 2.; "spiritual" was added by NVOAD.

[3]*Long Term Recovery Guide,* NVOAD, Dec. 2012, 6.
[4]For more information about spiritual and emotional Care, see Section 4 of this book: Providing the Eye in the Storm: Perspectives on Psychosocial Care and Disaster Response.

Chapter 11: How Vulnerable Populations Are Affected by Disasters

[1]From http://www.unisdr.org/we/coordinate/hfa

Chapter 12: Environmental Issues and Disaster Recovery

[1]From http://www.usgbc.org/leed
[2]From http://www.greensburggreentown.org
[3]From http://www.nccecojustice.org

Chapter 14: The Importance of Spiritual and Emotional Care

[1]National Voluntary Organizations Active in Disaster Points of Consensus (Disaster Spiritual Care) – http://www.nvoad.org.

Chapter 15: What Faith Communities Need to Know

[1]Harold Kushner, *When Bad Things Happen to Good People* (1981; New York: Anchor, 2004), 144.
[2]A.J. Weaver, H.G. Koenig, and F.M. Ochberg, "Posttraumatic stress, mental health professionals, and the clergy: A need for collaboration, training, and research," *Journal of Traumatic Stress,* 9 (1996): 847–56.
[3]Ibid.
[4]J.M. Schultz, Z. Espinel, S. Galea, I.A. Shaw, amd G.T. Miller, *Surge, Sort, Support: Disaster Behavioral Health for Health Care Professionals* (Miami: DEEP Center, University of Miami, Miller School of Medicine, 2006).
[5]National Institute of Mental Health, *Evidence-Based Early Psychological Intervention for Victims/Survivors of Mass Violence: A Workshop to Reach Consensus on Best Practices,* NIH Publication No. 02-5138 (Washington, D.C.: U.S. Government Printing Office, 2002).
[6](Center for the Study of Traumatic Stress, 2005; as cited in Schultz et al., 2006).
[7](NIMH, 2001).
[8]National Institute of Mental Health, *Evidence-Based Early Psychological Intervention.*
[9]National Center for PTSD, *Pharmacological Treatment of Acute Stress Reactions and PTSD: A Fact Sheet For Providers* (2008). Available at http://www.ptsd.va.gov/professional/pages/fslist-tx-overview.asp. Accessed August 31, 2012.
[10]J. Matt, (2009, updated 2012). National Center for PTSD, *Clinician's Guide to Medications for PTSD.* Available at http://www.ptsd.va.gov/professional/pages/clinicians-guide-to-medications-for-ptsd.asp. Accessed Sept 3, 2012.
[11]J.I. Bisson, A. Ehlers, R. Matthews, S. Pilling, D. Richards, and S. Turner, "Psychological treatments for chronic post-traumatic stress disorder," *British Journal of Psychiatry* (2007): 97–104.
[12]B.O. Rothbaum, M.C. Kearns, M. Price, E. Malcoun, M. Davis, K.J. Ressler, D. Lang, D. Houry, "Early Intervention May Prevent the Development of Posttraumatic Stress Disorder: A Randomized Pilot Civilian Study with Modified Prolonged Exposure," *Biological Psychiatry* (July 2012) PMID: 22766415.
[13]S. Satel, and S.O. Lilienfeld, *Brainwashed: The Seductive Appeal of Mindless Neuroscience* (New York: Basic Books, 2013).
[14]E.B. Foa, T.M. Keane, M.J. Friedman, and J.A. Cohen, eds., *Effective Treatments for PTSD: Practice Guide-lines from the International Society for Traumatic Stress Studies,* 2d ed. (New York: Guilford Press, 2009).
[15]Weaver et al, "Posttraumatic stress."
[16]S. Lilienfeld, S. Lynn, and J. Lohr, *Science and Pseudoscience in Clinical Psychology* (New York: Guilford Press, 2004).

[17]D. Meichenbaum, *Trauma, spirituality and recovery: Toward a spiritually-integrated psychotherapy* (2008). Retrieved from http://www.melissainstitute.org/documents/ SPIRITUALITY_PSYCHOTHERAPY.pdf. Accessed Sept 1, 2012.

[18]Foa et al., "Effective Treatments"

[19]Kushner, *When Bad Things Happen*, 150.

Chapter 17: "Hurt People Hurt Other People"

[1]M. Cabrera, "Living and Surviving in a Multiply Wounded Country," http://www. envio.org/ni/articulo/1629.

[2]Carolyn Yoder, "Trauma-Sensitive Development and Aid," in *Monthly Developments Magazine, InterAction*, Washington, D.C., pp. 22–23.

[3]Ibid.

[4]Ibid.

[5]Much of the information in the next section comes from an interview of Elaine Zook Barge by Yago Abeledo, http://www.breathingforgiveness.net/2013/04/anti-slavery-campaign-interview-series.html.

[6]Levine, Peter, "Why We Need Emotional First Aid," at http://www.traumahealing. com/somatic-experiencing/guide-to-help-cope-after-tragedy-accidents-death.html.

[7]Carolyn E. Yoder and E. Z. Barge, *STAR: The Unfolding Story, 2001–2011* (Harrisonburg, Va.: Eastern Mennonite University, 2011), 4–7.

[8]D. P. Aldrich, "How to Weather a Hurricane," *The New York Times*, August 29, 2012, p. A27.

[9]Special thanks to Dr. Vernon Jantzi of the STAR team for his assistance with this article. The STAR team is available to collaborate with organizations working with communities experiencing current or historical trauma from natural disaster, violence, or sustained poverty.

Chapter 18: Building Networks and Utilizing Community Resources

[1]National Research Council, *Disaster Resilience: A National Imperative* (Washington, D.C.: The National Academies Press, 2012).

[2]CWE Emergency Response Specialists deploy to provide training in best practices for long-term recovery groups and can often secure grants to support the work. These recovery groups bring together community and government resources to ensure that everyone has a chance to recover. For more information, visit http://www.cwsglobal.org/what-we-do/ emergencies/us-emergency-response/erp-staff.html.

Chapter 20: Denominational Offices and Parachurch Organizations

[1]The link to UMCOR's training menu and request form is http://www.umcor. org/UMCOR/Programs/Disaster-Response/US-Disaster-Response/Training/Training. The training calendar is also available at http://www.umcor.org/UMCOR/Programs/ Disaster-Response/Training-Calendar/Training-Calendar

[2]Like dioceses, synods, or presbyteries in other denominations, conferences are the judicatory bodies that connect general church agencies with local churches in a particular area. Each United Methodist congregation exists within a district and conference, presided over by a bishop. When UMCOR offers training, mentoring, or funding, it does so through a request from within the conference.

Printed in the USA
CPSIA information can be obtained
at www.ICGtesting.com
LVHW081747031123
762986LV00046B/1063